Joy In the Journey

The Journey In

Inspiring and restoring Joy in the face of adversity.

Joy In The Journey by Shaylon Ware

Published in the United States by Shaylon Ware Global Ministries, an imprint of the ICM International Publishing Group, a division of ICM International Inc.

996 Maine Ave SW #417, Washington, DC 20024

www.liveicm.org or telephone number (202-683-9672)

Copyright © 2020 by Shaylon Ware.

Visit the Author's website at www.shaylonware.com

All rights reserved.

Library of Congress Cataloging-in-Publication Data:

Ware, Shaylon B.

Good Morning Joy / Shaylon B. Ware. First Edition. pages cm

Includes bibliographical references.

ISBN 978-1-7378906-0-7(trade paper)

1. Spirituality 2. Self-Help. 3. Prayer

Cover Design by Ashley Johnson Cross

All materials written are protected by copyright laws and are owned by author. No use or publication of material (printed, electronic, or otherwise) without prior written permission of publisher, except as provided by United States of America copyright law. Unless otherwise noted, all Scripture quotations are from the King James Version of the Bible.

While the author has made every effort to provide accurate telephone numbers and Internet addresses at the time of publication, neither the publisher nor the author assumes any responsibility for errors or for changes that occur after publication.

Dedication

This book is dedicated to my reason, my son Jalen, who has always encouraged me to have "childlike faith."

To know you Jalen is to love you. You are a young man of few words but when you speak; your words are full of life and wisdom. You are the center of my calm and a jewel in my crown. You are absolutely, positively the core of my heart. I love you entirely son! I thought for many years as your mother, that I kept you alive (inside joke) but in reality, it was you who kept me living! A man of integrity, respect, kindness and greatness, yes you are!

I will never forget the evening a special birthday party that was being held in my honor. Many had spoken beautiful words and your time to share had come. You said, "Mom, you are so awesome. But it's like everyone sees it. Everyone knows it but you." I couldn't understand at the time, why you waited to tell me something so private at such a public affair. These words have lived hidden away in my heart since then. I understand now Jalen.

You have and continue to be someone who truly sees me, and it was through your eyes, I was finally able to see what you see….the awesomeness of ME!

Thank you Son, my best-est best-est!

Always remember, you are a King!

Acknowledgements

To my Mother, Veneta Ruth Spicer for introducing me to the true meaning of holiness and modeling love.

To my Brother, Terrance Russell & Sister Charday Russell, forever and always you have my heart.

To my Aunt, Letha Deon Allen for all the realest heart to heart, woman to woman talks.

To my Aunt & God Mother, Henrietta Anderson for always being there.

To my Aunt May Otis Russell, for crossing the finish line with us; my angel.

I do not have the words to describe how much I love each of you. Thank you. A special thank you to my family and friends. I love and appreciate you.

P.S.

To every reader,

Thank you for the love you've shown, the support you've given and the time you've taken to read my first of many books to come! I am truly grateful to God for you. I pray you were blessed and that you journey with JOY!

Sincerely, with love

God bless you,

S.B.W.

FOREWORD

To my Daughter Shaylon Brena Ware,

I am so proud of you. God gave you a purpose and you are a powerful and anointed woman for the kingdom of God. You are a positive influence for young women's lives and all women. God has given you a vision for this time and season. The things you have accomplished in life were by nobody but God. The love you have for your son, Jalen Wilson and seeing about him and taking care of me in this season with stage 4 invasive lobular carcinoma (breast cancer), and you have stood by me. You don't work to take care of me and take me back and forth to see doctors (MRI, CT Scans) and letting me stay at your home. Both you and your sister Charday came up with a plan that would work!

In this journey we pray and have faith in God and his love that he has for us. There is joy, peace, strength in him. Shaylon, you were praying miracles, signs and wonders and that's what we are standing on for our family. Love you Shaylon. The doors are opening in this season for you, the platform has been set. Walk on it! It is your time!

Love you Shaylon,

Your Mother, Veneta Spicer.

CONTENTS

	PREFACE	
Chapter 1:	The Power Of Choice	14
Chapter 2:	Now Walk It Out	23
Chapter 3:	Don't Believe The Hype	29
Chapter 4:	It's All Good	35
Chapter 5:	To Be Rich	41
Chapter 6:	Won't He do It	47
Chapter 7:	You Will Know	54
Chapter 8:	What Do You See?	61
Chapter 9:	Come Thirsty	66
Chapter 10:	Customized Blessing	71
Chapter 11:	You've Been Set Up	78
Chapter 12:	Belief for Your Unbelief	86
Chapter 13:	Just a Lil Talk with Jesus	93
Chapter 14:	Be Great	100
Chapter 15:	Joy In The Rain	110

Testimony: Henrietta Anderson, Deon Allen

Authors Bio & Testimony

PREFACE

In 2016 I launched a blog from the pages of my journal entitled *Joy in the Journey*. The objective was to chronologically transcribe my journey in discovering and reclaiming a lost treasure; Joy. I'm not sure at what point I lost it or if there was some cataclysmic event that was the finale of what was once the champion of my strength. Or had it been a slow sequential process, like a full glass imperfect by a mere superficial crack that over time leaked its contents upon the surfaces of life encounters. The blog was supposed to be a means to an end, compiled journal entries of many encouraging topics and revelations that aided myself and others in identifying thieves to thriving and maintaining their joy overall!

Unbeknownst to me, the blog was simply the concierge during my journey to emotional and interpersonal healing. A greater purpose emerged. In my attempts to capture joy, I began a journey of self-discovery, adventure, exploration and arrived at self-love! It is very possible despite living with yourself to not know thyself, under qualifying the impact of our supernatural encounters as supernatural beings by measuring ourselves next to our humanistic experiences. It is quite possible to be more intimately acquainted with external fixtures such as relationships, roles, functions and possessions than we are with internal components such as our own spirit, soul and body.

Why is that so? How is it that we are these uniquely designed hand crafted masterpieces, the expressed breath of Almighty God in like-ness and image with unlimited favor, indispensable power both in heaven and earth, immutable Kingdom DNA through the blood of Jesus Christ, who are loved relentlessly, redeemed eternally, accepted graciously and mercifully; how is it that we still don't know who we are?

The fruit of who we are sprouts from the root of our faith! It was nearly impossible for me to maintain the fruit of the Spirit:

Joy, when the root of my Faith image was malnourished. I discuss how to break perpetuating negative cycles and create new themes, and how to address false beliefs and adopting truth in the chapter "Belief for My Unbelief", "Be Great", "and The Power of Choice".

I recall being an avid journalist (my imagination, emotions and experiences only). Often what was too taboo or cliché to be said in an open forum was always acceptable and "erasable" in the vaulted lines of my journal! There were long seasons of writing and rewriting, much of which I wouldn't relive if it were optional but I remember these same seasons being my healthiest because I was true to self. I had a place where "no holds bar" was standard. Like a pen in the hand of a ready writer, always much to caption I carried my journal everywhere. One time I lost my journal. I spent days looking for it and realized I had left it at the church. Instantly I couldn't breathe. All my indecencies, transgressions not to mention my most cherished secrets were left on a church bench waiting to be read as a $5.00 tabloid. I could see the headliner now, "Holy or Hot Mess that is the Question"! If your journal is anything like mine, its pages are peaks and pits of the many highways of your heart, random adventures, sentences that end abruptly without completion, illegible handwriting that at this point you can't make out what was even written.

What about the pages stained with tears, make-up blotches, and the infamous coffee or food art? Let's call it just that... art! I'd be remiss to leave out the prayers and scriptures. What makes the journey of a journal so personal is that it's life on a line, literally. Things that you may never reveal to any living being, some of us have pets that know more about us than any human we interact with! Uncannily the journal unable to object, discriminate, break silence or run away keeps our best secrets. I'm sure there are people paying hundreds of dollars for therapy when a journal might do the job!

As healthy and therapeutic as journaling may be, it's not so much if that's where your essence is hidden. There are those who are freer on the line of their journal than they actually are in life. They say the best information is not by word of mouth but rather in a book. By nature a journal is supposed to be for an audience of one, secluded and placed out of reach, to be safe guarded. But what if every once in a while, instead of given someone access to the pages, you gave them access to the person writing the pages! What if we took somewhat random "entries" of life and let them live out loud! I'm not saying disregard the sanctity of the treasured relationship between the journey and the journal as a dramatization such as "Journal Tells All" but I am saying sometimes what goes in must come out! Some secrets need to be shared. Some parts of your journey need to become as visual as a motion picture. Everyone loves a good underdog story where the triumphant victory is saved the best for last!

So much of who I am was written, but never animated; after all who lets someone read their journal aloud right! I've learned that a component of Joy is exactly that, aloud. I am not referencing an audible loud sound as I am the notable frequency and energy of Joy! Joy is audacious, attractive and clearly resonates! There were many years that my Joy was either suppressed, repressed or nonexistent. Broken heart, betrayal, yes it is all a part of my journey to wholeness, acceptance and liberty! I hadn't always lived with pain. I hadn't always found solace in silence. I hadn't always wept more than I laughed or kept a distance to protect myself. Where did my joy retreat to? When did the fire and desire simmer? I was running well, who hindered me? Why did I begin to look again? In the journey inward I found those answers! We don't have to live guarded, hidden away like a history book on a shelf when there is so much joy to living a life expressly written and expressly animated.

There are many journeys we will embark upon as we embrace new beginnings, endings and at the very least growth. I believe somehow we have been trained to journey well outwardly without much consideration for what is required to journey well inwardly.

Isaiah 35:10 says "and those the Lord has rescued will return. They will enter Zion with singing; everlasting joy will crown their heads. Gladness and joy will overtake them, and sorrow and sighing will flee away! That's exactly what The Journey In is! The journey of being rescued and returning to our rightful posture, Christ-like image and crown of everlasting joy & gladness!

A few years back I was offered an opportunity of a lifetime to go to Ghana, West Africa for two weeks. Prior to the offer I had a vivid dream. In the dream I was dressed in African clothing in a coliseum, in the nosebleed section. Looking downward I seen hundreds of empty seats, a stage and several entryways. Although no one was in the coliseum, I could see people flooding in. I felt a sense of urgency to get to the stage. In the dream I knew the people flooding in were there because there was something I was supposed to do. They were there for me. The dream was so tangibly real that I shared it with a friend for clarity. Weeks later a missionary called me whom I hadn't had much contact with prior, asked if I had ever considered international travel or missions. She proceeded to tell me about an upcoming mission trip to Africa and she was led by the Holy Spirit to contact me in hopes that I would attend. It had already been confirmed in my spirit that it was my season to go. We both began to cry we were so excited and we ended the call in prayer. Over the next few months we made preparations for the extensive trip. Initially the preparatory items were all external such as fundraising, gathering donations and items to carry with, obtaining sponsors and engaging our community for support. The trip was costly and steadily we received money up until the week before departure. However, the external preparation was not nearly as time consuming as the internal. As the trip date approached, we began having weekly conference call meetings, with assignments of prayer and fasting, we were required to have a medical checkup and shots to safeguard our immune system while overseas. Bishop Simms, our missions guide and facilitator was very direct and supplied as much information as possible so that we would be informed about the culture, the people and what to expect. Yet, how do you mentally prepare to journey to a place you have never been.

Your spirit can and will journey far beyond your consciousness, while extending provisional space and grace for your physical being to catch up! My spirit had already aligned with the journey to Africa but I needed to prepare naturally. I began waking up early hours for prayer to avoid severe jetlag, I read about their customs and language. I watched videos and such. The greatest effort was preparing myself mentally to serve in a country with extreme needs.

Upon our arrival we were given devotional assignments and placed into teams to aid the efforts of our mission's trip. Every morning we met an hour before breakfast to pray, study the word of God and worship. The purpose of the morning ritual was to bring solidarity and unity to us as a team, to provide stabilization and assurance. We had to touch the heart of God before we were enabled to touch the heart of man. We were formidable and graced with sustenance for the day.

It was the most impactful, life changing experience. Since then I have travelled internationally several times in less than three years for ministry and service. However, my travels to discover and embrace other truths and my identity were far reaching and more extensive than any third-world country I have visited.

Similar to the trips you make daily, as minute as journeying to work to journeying through a life transition such as marriage or retirement, internal preparation is key. It starts with a decision to take the journey, go on the trip. Along the way the journey into self may prove difficult having to face the unexpected hurdles of your personality & erroneous beliefs about self, unpacking unhealthy habits, learning how to maneuver reroutes of dreams and expectations, doing the dirty work of switching out flat tires when there is a blow out of emotion, finding other avenues to avoid dead ends and road blocks such as fear, insecurity and discouragement. The journey inward seldom lends itself to shortcuts when it comes to soul work however there are pot holes and gravel roads you will bypass when you discover you've been that way before and didn't arrive at your desired destination! New terrains and landscapes of who you are and were created to be will be so refreshing and enlightening!

The journey in is not so much about the arrival as it is the journey. We can have joy overall in our journey to becoming and fulfilling our destiny! The choice has always been ours to make.

Joy Overall is Yours!

1 The Power of Choice

Take your personal power back! Seize it. The choice has always been yours.

I will never forget that moment in the midst of chaos, engaged in the ugly cry. You know, the type of crying where you can no longer breathe out of your nose, your eyes nearly swollen shut, lips have dried out at this point... yeah, not the loud attention grabbing cry, but that deep silent, can't do anything but shake and whimper cry. The Spirit of the Lord said, "Choose Joy". "Seriously God? Just like that, just choose?" I thought.

Who knew? Seriously who knew that Joy was a decision, a choice? To some the option to choose, be it an emotion or response, may appear to be an obvious one. Not so much for others, including myself at one time. The revelation was a life changing moment, like one of those ah-ha Oprah moments! As I reflected on the truth that he gave me the power to choose and the choice was mine; I made a decision to take my personal power back, to stop crying over things I had the power to change. I chose life over death, victory over defeat, positive over negative, abundance over scarcity, prosperity over poverty, wholeness over weakness and Joy over sorrow!

I recall often stating how individuals made me feel, as if they had the power to manipulate and control my emotions, the functional capacity of the inner workings of my heart. I recall stating "You made me feel", which denotes their authority and power over my own will. Now this may not be as indicting when the emotion is esteeming such as romance or flattery. Nevertheless, the contrasting emotion of rejection or inferiority in whatever way experienced can be rendered powerless. It is very possible to deny the influence and infiltration of any emotion. Ownership of your state of mind or emotional status deters projection and blame of others. Power is dually operative. Power can be given or taken, relinquished or restrained. We determine its administration and operation.

I was working with an all teen girls group. With this particular group I provided Counseling and empowerment support, mentorship and leadership. These young ladies come from a triage of dysfunctional backgrounds. Many of whom were orphans, abandoned by their parents as a result of systemic drug use and criminal activity. I will never forget one girl in particular; we will call her "Sabrina". Sabrina was new to the girl's transitional home. This particular session topic was self-esteem. We always start the class with an activity that is related to the topic. On this day we opened the class with an improv runway. The girls were placed into groups of three and were given material to design an outfit for one of their group members. They had to work together to design the outfit, while the third member had to wear the outfit and model it on the runway. The personalities of some of the girls were like placing superstars in front of a camera while others avoided the attention. One by one each group cheered for their model. The room was filled with laughter and creativity! Afterward, I discussed with the girls about how they felt during the activity.

Many of them had several positive things to say, but Sabrina, avoiding the discussion appeared frustrated and angry. When I asked her what she was feeling, she began to disclose how she didn't feel the same positive energy as some of the other girls. Sabrina had been separated from her mother due to abuse in the household. She began to repeat horrific things that had been said to her that smeared her self-image. It was nearly impossible at this point for Sabrina to look at me. The more she spoke of how she was made to feel by others that had harmed her, the angrier she became. Her face flushed, tears cascading, and her arms folded in defense; my heart began to break. I realized in that very moment, that this beautiful girl's personal power was taken from her and anger was her only comfort.

I said, "Sabrina, what if I told you, that you have the power to decide what you feel and what you believe?" Looking down, crying and shaking her head in complete resistance, she became even more upset and said "No, people say whatever they want to you and when they do you can't control how you feel." My next question was, "Could it be that you can't control how you feel because a part of you believes what is being said to you?" She began to cry harder. I asked her to look at me, she refused. For several moments I challenged her to look at me, and finally her eyes met mine and I began to tell her the opposite of every negative thing she had been told about herself. The moment was so intense that other girls in the group began to cry, a gripping hush filled the room as Sabrina and I worked through identifying and uprooting the false beliefs she'd adopted as her truth and had been rehearsing, repeatedly beating herself down with. When I finished, she peacefully dropped her head and said, "Wow, I haven't been able to look anybody in the eyes in years, but I believed what you were saying, so I could." I reiterated to her that again it was her choice to believe me, just as she had the lies. It had always been her right to choose calm rather than the rage. When she realized she had the power, her entire countenance shifted and mindset elevated! We had several conversations later and she became one of my most memorable students.

This experience seemed to be life changing for her. As a result, I was provoked time and time again to choose what I would believe, choose my emotions, choose my attitude, and choose the thoughts I would entertain and accept as truth. The implementation of "minding my mind" or in others words, think about what it is that you are thinking about became a daily exercise. Managing your mind includes renewing your mind. Replacing old negative thoughts with new positive thoughts, but positive thinking is not enough. Renewing the mind means transforming the mind! Habits, routines, belief systems alike, it is not the learning of something new, but unlearning what has been taught or learned! Changing and exchanging does not come without difficulty, but it is achievable daily with the word and commitment to the process. These choices had to be independent of my environment or the expectation of others. I had to choose for me without consideration of circumstance! I'll be honest; if you hadn't made this a common practice, choosing "up" can be extremely difficult when the law of gravity is determined to pull you down! The choice is just the beginning. Once the choice is made, action is to follow. Often the action is the direct opposite of the opposition. Choosing to laugh rather than cry. Have you ever started laughing to keep from crying? Yeah, awkward at first right!! The power to choose, free will remains one of the greatest assets of our humanity! Jesus himself said "You have not chosen me, but I chose you. John 15:16.

God gave us power and freedom of choice. Choice implies preference. Consider your abilities? Ability implies action. What power have you given away that you need to take back?

In order for you to choose, options and opportunity must first be made available. How could you choose love if the option to hate wasn't a possibility? Each of us is afforded options in regard to self-will. Choice implies preference. In others words, when you "select" whatever it is you "choose" it implies that this is your PREFERENCE. Take a moment and reflect on some recent choices you've made?

Was that your preference? What about the outcome, did you get what you preferred? I just had a flash back of some "associations" that I did not really prefer but I chose. Believe me, it was a misinformed choice. All the information was based on lies and flesh-inspired. Yet had I known the truth, I might have made a different choice. Then there are those choices made from uninhibited desire. We want what we want, when we want it and the consequences are subsequently damaging. This is often times the case when we choose the alternative to God's will.

Let's look at the vocabulary:

Power: the ability to do something or act in a particular way, or quality. 2 the capability or ability to direct or influence behavior or the course of events. To enact or perform with strength, might or force.., the possession of control or command.

Choice: An act of selecting, making a decision when faced with two or more possibilities. Option, alternative, possible course of action, an opportunity to choose.

The phrase "Knowledge is power" is attributed to Sir. Francis Bacon who agreed that with knowledge our potential & abilities improve our quality of life. Scripture by which we have knowledge of God, depicts him giving us the power (for reference: knowledge) to choose and make informed choices through his word. Joshua 24:15 "choose you this day whom ye will serve", Deut. 30:19 "therefore choose life that both thou and thy seed may live'. Psalm 119:30 David said," I have chosen the way of truth."

You shall KNOW the truth and the truth shall make you free (John 8:32)... KNOWING truth is the prerequisite of knowing freedom!

It is not intended for us to choose without wisdom, knowledge or understanding. Even when we don't know all the details, it is the power and knowledge of his word, by faith that sustains our commitment to that which we choose. Power in itself without knowledge and faith, is mere force without control. God would have us to make informed choices based on truth, for intended results! He's intentional and so should we be as his sons and daughters!

We have been given the power to choose Rejoicing over Rejection, Faith over Fear, Construction over Destruction, Mercy over Malice, and Grace over Gossip!

Have you ever had to make a decision between two options? Have you ever had the Lord give you instruction without explanation? You may not know exactly what to do, how to do it or even why, but knowledge of his word will influence your persuasion. His word today is rejoice always (Phil 4:4) count it all joy (James 1:2:3). The attributes of God are within you. He has given you all things pertaining to godliness. You're not just anybody, but a Queen of the King, someone of royal stature! You're too big to think small, and too high to settle for low! Choose. Make the decision that from today onward you will not give power to anything that is detrimental to your Joy. One challenge amongst some women, is feeling guilty or "selfish" for choosing "self". The greatest needs we have are often the same needs we ourselves are providing for in others. Being nurturers by nature, we tend to take in anything, anyone and any project that needs a "nest" leaving ourselves with no place to rest. Self-care is the best care. Self-love is unselfish love, and it's biblical! We must love our neighbors as we love ourselves, not instead of ourselves! Choosing you does not mean excluding others, it means including you!

Choosing to say "no" is a healthy yes in reverse! Just because you can do it, doesn't mean you should do it! There are roles you will need to retire in order to accommodate the spiritual development God desires to mature in you. Within you, there are treasures, every fruit of the spirit and much more. It is a choice to allow the diamond to shine or remain buried in the shaft. It is a choice to walk in pity or power. The word applies to battles within and the battles without, both of which you've been given power to win! That area where you have given over your personal power to appease the needs of others should be revisited, unless of course doing so brings you **JOY!**

So what am I saying? POWER & CHOICE: Ability, Influence, Strength, Decision, Possession, Control and Opportunity....

Nehemiah 8:10 ..." this day is holy to our Lord: Do not grieve for the joy of the Lord is your strength. (NIV)

1 Thess. 5:16."Rejoice evermore. (KJV)

God would not ask you to produce something you didn't already possess! He would not ask you to manifest anything he hadn't manufactured! You possess the ability and strength to positively influence your life through the opportunity of choice! You have the power. The choice is yours.

Much like Sabrina, the rehearsal of negative thoughts, events, stories or experiences will deplete and ultimately dominate your joy, self-worth, confidence, and ability to receive that which is good. I am not diminishing any of my experiences or yours for that matter, but there comes a time when you have to get a new story or at least tell your story from a different vantage point! Yes, it was traumatic but the moment of trauma does not have to enslave your present or future. That traumatic experience can be repurposed to serve as aid in the lives of others.

The power of our emotions is subservient to the ruling power of our thoughts. Choose according to what you know rather than what you feel! Our Thoughts instigate our emotions, our emotions perpetuate our actions. The power of choice truly begins and ends in the framework of our mentality.

Practice Minding Your Mind:

1. Pay attention to what you are thinking about. (Mind Management)
2. Is the thought yours and if so, where did it originate?
3. Is the thought fact or truth?
4. Confront your thoughts by challenging them with the word of God.
5. Cast them down and take them captive.
6. Replace any false thought/belief with truth.
7. Choose based on Truth! And it's okay to choose YOU!

2 Now Walk It Out

I'd rather be the head of a chicken, doing something great while being small; then be the tail of a bull, being small following behind someone great.

Walk It Out!

Over time one block increased to 2 miles per day. Walking was my time of meditation, an opportunity to walk out my thoughts and pray. Initially, after the first few blocks I would wipe sweat from my brow, gulp invisible buckets of air and my thighs would itch with madness. Maybe stretching first would have alleviated the discomfort. Then I learned even stretching can be difficult if the body, frame of mind has not been conditioned to be repositioned. I hope you caught that thought! Although the act of walking was common; to walk as a calculated, faith based, mentally engaged activity was new.

2 Corinthians 5:7 (KJV) For we walk by faith, not by sight... (MSG) It's what we trust in but do not yet see that keeps us going. Do you suppose a few ruts in the road or rocks in the path are going to stop us? No.

Let's look at the vocabulary: *Walk*

- OT & NT Biblical reference/ verb: Walk- (metaphorical) to follow a certain path or course of life; to conduct oneself in a certain way.
- Greek New Testament/Present tense- a continued mode of conduct or behavior. The infinitive "to walk" can be translated "To Live".
- To advance, proceed by steps, advancing the feet alternately so that there is always one foot on the ground
- the effect of alternate expansion or contraction; to proceed through, over or upon at a moderate pace

I love the transitional language of "to walk" also means to Live! I'd like to pause and ask you a question.

Are you living? Is the life you are living today what you hope to behold tomorrow?

Does your action match your words and your hope? *The distinction between hope and faith is that faith is now. Hope is then, held in the grip of the future.* Take a moment to reflect upon what it is that you hope for. Is there a correlation between speech, deed and scripture? Are you demonstrating what you are anticipating?

Demonstrate. Both naturally and spiritually, you must demonstrate. We must walk out our confessions of faith. Let your speech, actions and deeds correspond with what you believe, including scripture. Your faith will be stretched by struggle and success. The day may come when you may not be so inclined to walk in peace with your adversary, but live peaceably as much as lies within you anyway (Romans 12:18). Walk It Out. The moment may come when you've forgotten the sound of a new song, but sing to the Lord a new song, sing anyway (Psalm 96:1). Walk It Out. Dark clouds may rise; stormy winds may blow, but lift up your eyes to the hills from where your help comes, look up anyway. Keep moving one step at a time. Demonstrate that which you anticipate. His word is a lamp unto our feet and a light unto our path and a righteous man's steps are ordered by the Lord. I am reminded of an old song called Order My Steps.

Order my steps in your word dear Lord

Lead me, guide me every day

Send your anointing Father I pray

Order my steps in your word

Please order my steps in your word

To walk it out is to LIVE. Walk out every victory and every promise. Blow ye the trumpet and sound the alarm that there is abundance in every area of your life! Let your praise rise with thanksgiving and adoration for the marvelous things he's done, doing and will do! Walk out every fiber of your faith. Every step taken is territory taken! A wise old mother would say you have to crawl before you walk. In Jesus name we are no longer gripping the carpet as infants but rather the hand of God, taking large steps, moving forward by leaps and bounds!

Many scriptures reference "running", "run" or "race" in comparison to life, pace and time. Isaiah 40:31 for example, "They that wait upon the Lord shall renew their strength. They shall mount up with wings as eagles; they shall run and not be weary, and they shall walk and not faint."

We are travelers striving to make the best of our journey. Let us resolve to walk in the steps of faith (Romans 4:12) toward every promise. The Lord has granted us divine grace that enables us to do so and find comfort in him while we journey.

John 12:35-36 (KJV) Walk while you have the light. While you have the light believe in the light. Who is the LIGHT? Jesus Christ.

Let this be your confidence: He who has promised is faithful and not just faithful but true. He is faithful and true and he walks with you as he did with Noah, Enoch and Abraham. He will send his angel with you to make your joy of salvation a journey that is filled with pleasure, and his spirit is ever present to guide. What a mighty God we serve! Keep advancing, expanding, proceeding; Keep living. You may ask what I do mean by "it? Whatever your "it" is, do it. Walk out your destiny. Walk out your prayers. Walk out your purpose. Walk out the word. Walk out his promises! Work with what you have and it will work for you in the end! It's not how you start but how you finish.

There is absolutely nothing wrong with preparing for your walk with a stretch! That time of preparation positions you mentally for the steps ahead. I have never seen a newborn enter the world running with Nike shoes on. The process of walking out ordained steps of the Lord often start with baby steps, beginner steps of hope! As you walk, you are inadvertently training to LEAP!

I had no idea I was being conditioned to be repositioned. Rejection conditioned me to be a true friend and a compassionate servant. Lack conditioned me to be a wise steward of my time, talents and possessions. Brokenness conditioned me to be humble yet assured. Walking out of something is many times more impactful than walking into something! What you walked away from granted access and opportunity for you to walk into something new!

Staying too long is just as detrimental as leaving too early! At some point you will have to walk it out!

You can walk out of pain, frustration, disappointment, hopelessness. You can walk away from unhealthy relationships, toxic connections and contracts! You can walk off a dead end job, dead end assignment, dead end position and walk into alignment, fulfillment, agreement and destiny!

Everything you have endured walking into and walking out of was or is a part of the conditioning process! On this journey you've increased endurance to see things through until the end. You've gained agility, the ability to make moves without toil or hardness easily and swiftly. Get up and keep moving. You're headed somewhere beyond your wildest dreams!

Be encouraged in the journey, and know that it is the Lord, himself who goes before you and will be with you. He will never leave you nor forsake you. Do not be afraid; do not be discouraged. (Deut. 31:8). It is for what is unseen, that we press.

3 Don't Believe the Hype

It's not over until the fat lady sings. I've actually met her. She has chronic laryngitis!

"Yeah boy" was his hashtag line. He was a natural at exciting the crowd. Loud. Flamboyant. Larger than life personality. Over the top. Hyper. If his colorful clothing or crazed style of dancing didn't get your attention, that gaudy clock around his neck sure did! We know him as "Flavor Flav", the hype man for hip hop group Public Enemy. Behind the scene William Jonathan Drayton Jr. was a man that battled crack cocaine addiction, alcoholism, domestic violence and crime. Despite his public hype, he battled a private enemy.

With all we have observed in recent social media and television, displays of injustice, natural disaster, hostility and economic decline the testimony of Christian faith and love, may to some appear to be a defeated sector. Yet, I must say this, "DONT BELIEVE THE HYPE." Yes, we have an enemy, Satan (John 10:10). However, we must remember as the secular world publicly hypes his tactics and devices; he is a liar and the truth is not in him (John 8:44). Our God and his word is true. He is defeated and it was our God who defeated him (Revelation 12:10).

"Discipline yourselves, keep alert. Like a roaring lion your adversary the devil prowls around, looking for someone to devour. Resist him, steadfast in your faith...." (1 Peter 5:8-9 NRSV). Don't confuse the liar with the Lion. Satan is described "as" a lion. This is a depiction of his disposition not his position of power. There is yet one, who is all powerful, a lone Lion worthy of recognition and praise, who has dominion and authority. He is the Lion of Judah, One who is called the Lion and the Lamb, our Savior and Lord, Jesus Christ. He is the Truth. He is our Lord and King. He reigns supreme. His name is above all names. He is worthy of not hype, but honor.

Lets look at the vocabulary: *Hype vs Honor (Merriam Webster)*

- **Hype:** extravagant or intensive publicity or promotion of exaggerated claims, exaggeration of importance or benefits, a fad, a strategy for marketing.

- **Honor:** One whose worth brings respect or fame. Public esteem, merited respect, a person of superior standing, a privilege, distinction, recognition of glory, prestige or admiration.

The Lion is established and distinct in honor, while the liar is esteemed and depicted through hype.

The hype of gain, fashion, "the hustle & flow", the theatrics or production of our flesh does not excite neither honor God. All that this world offers and its presentations will inevitably pass. The glory of his name and honor of his prestige shall remain.

I choose to honor God! Let us choose to render him authentic, wholly, superior devotion through righteous living and exuberant worship & praise, rather than being coerced and seduced by the hype of this world. Worldly hype would suggest and promote an exaggerated contradiction of all that God has spoken and demonstrated. Our God, our King, our Lion of the tribe of Judah is awesome! The Lion does not need a hype man; for the basis of hype is exaggeration. How could we possibly exaggerate on the magnificence of God? Everything about our God is extravagant! He's just that supremely adorned! He is astounding, eminent, forbearing, gracious, and incorruptible and the list goes on! To speak of his fame and glory is infinite in measure. A thousand tongues wouldn't touch the surface of his excellence!

He said to me, I AM GOD......

I am God, God of miracles, signs, wonders, I am Healer, I am matchless and Master. I am protector and the answer. I am listening and attentive to your call. I remember. I am impeccable, kind, merciful, forgiving, long-suffering, and compassionate. I AM Love and continue to love without conditions. I am God... I am righteous ruler who restores. I am the one who is strong and mighty. I am the one who allows the sun to rise and the moon to set. I am he that gifted life, peace and all spiritual blessings.

It is my voice that calls the rivers and seas to flow within their borders. I am he that shares my breath with you daily. I am he who covers your head in the heat of day, and warms your soul in the winter season. I have not, will not and cannot fail. I am truth. I am life. I am able. The heavens declare my glory and the earth is arrayed in my splendor. I am King. I am Jehovah. Consider the work of my hands. Can they be numbered? Can my works be reversed? Ponder the depth of my mercy and grace. Can either be awarded by merit? I am God and I am always good.

It is the enemy's prerogative to persuade you into believing your labor has been in vain, that you have lost more than you've gained. His attempt to shame you with regret and bitterness, recession and regression are constructed smoke screens to distract and provoke concession and doubt. The reality is God said......

I AM and I WILL

Restore- I am the Lord your God and I will restore your fortunes (all that has been lost and stolen) and have

compassion on you. I will gather you and bring you back. You will possess that which I have promised you and I will make you more prosperous and numerous than those before you. Those who took advantage of you will be cursed. You shall reign and obey me and love the Lord with your whole heart. You will live. You will be abundantly prosperous in all your undertakings, in your body, livestock and land. I will take delight in prospering you.
(Deuteronomy 30: 1-13 paraphrased MSG)

Help- I am your refuge and strength a present help in the time of trouble, so do not fear, for I am with you; do not be dismayed, for I am your God. I will strengthen you and help you. I will uphold you with my righteous right hand. Cast your care on me and I will sustain you. I will never let the righteous be shaken. (Psalm 55:22 Psalm 46-1-3 Isaiah 41:10-13 MSG)

Heal- I am the Lord, your healer who will take away from you all sickness. I will bless your bread and your water, forgive all your iniquities and heal all your diseases. I bore your sins in my body on the tree, that you might die to sin and live to righteousness. By my wounds you have been healed. (Psalm 103: 1-3 Exodus 23: 25-25, Exodus 15:26 Peter 2:24 MSG)

Deliver- I am your rock, your fortress, and your deliverer; Your God, your strength in whom you trust I am your shield and the horn of your salvation and your stronghold (place of safety). I shall deliver you from the snare of the fowler and from the perilous pestilence. I am your hiding place and I will preserve you from trouble and I will surround you with songs of deliverance. I will deliver you from every evil work and preserve you for my heavenly Kingdom. (2 Samuel 22:2 Psalm 18: 1-2 Psalm 91:2-3 Psalm 32:7 2 Timothy 4:18)

Provide- I shall supply all your need according to my riches in glory by Christ Jesus. (Philippians 4:19)

Don't believe the hype, give God honor!

4 ITS ALL GOOD

Whoever said it's too good to be true, didn't know the truth.

The urban phrase "It's all good" has been coined with the origination by Bob Dylan as early as 1962, Richard Pryor and even MC Hammer as late as 1994. However, there is only one that has ultimate "dib's" on "It's All Good" and that's God! Yeah, they stole it! What is so amazing is that we now speak what he saw! What he saw, he first thought! Everything he thought was good therefore everything he made was good!

Genesis 1:26-31(paraphrased, NRSV) God said "Let us make humankind in our image, according to our likeness, and let them have dominion...So God created humankind in his image,...in the image of God he created them; male and female. God blessed them, and God said to them, "Be fruitful and multiply and fill the earth and subdue it and have dominion". God said, "See I have given you every plant and tree with seed in its fruit". God saw everything that he made, and indeed, it was very good.

In this passage of scripture there are 5 key "gifts" granted by the Father before the confirmation "It is indeed good".

1. Image 2. Dominion 3. Blessing 4. Duty 5. Provision

Let's look at the vocabulary: *Biblical Reference Dictionary & Meriam*

- **Image-** reflection, representation of spiritual personality and moral likeness, similitude or patterned after.
- **Dominion-** supremacy, complete authority, sovereignty, rule over, possession, power, jurisdiction, superiority or ascendancy.
- **Bless-** validate, confer or invoke divine favor upon, endow, consecrate.
- **Duty-** moral or, legal obligation, responsibility, and an action someone is required to perform.
- **Provision-** arrangement or preparation beforehand as for supplying or meeting a need.

I got excited just reading the definitions!

When God created us in his image and likeness, he was not referring to the physical stature of mankind, rather his character and personality; for God is a Spirit (John 4:24). The capacity to live righteously and benefit from fluid communication and fellowship with him.

The "image" of God, what does that look like to you?

Attributes & character of God entail faithful and true, strong and mighty, love and full of compassion, slow to anger and merciful, rich yet humble, Prince, ruler and shepherd.

Take a moment to name some things out loud that you know of him to be. Speak of his character.

In all that you have just spoken, would you believe that you possess the very same? You and I are as such because we were created by him, for him, like him and CHOOSE HIM! We are the sons and daughters of the Most High! Hallelujah! Because HE is, WE ARE also. Because He is, I am. The old folks used to say "the apple doesn't fall far from the tree."

Fill in the blank: "Because He is_____
_____
_____
I am_____
_____
_____.

Psalm 8:5-6: Yet you have made them a little lower than God, and crowned them with glory and honor. You have given them dominion over the works of your hands, you have put all things under their feet. (NSRV)

John 14:12: "Verily, verily I say unto you, He that believeth on me, the works that I do shall he do also; and greater works than these shall he do; because I go unto my Father." (KJV)

God gifted us with dominion to rule, to have complete authority in the earth, having put all things under our feet. We are superior to everything in and on the earth, with the exception of one another. This means every enemy, every diabolical trap or scheme; every persecutor and prosecutor is under your feet! Anything that you are above will remain beneath you. Scriptures tells us that we are above only and not beneath (Deut. 28:13). Bless God!

God is so awesome as if his image and the authority to have complete control over all the earth weren't enough; he then validates us with his blessing! As king scepter in hand, he extends approval with gesturing a tilted crown, our Father confers with himself, consecrates us and invokes divine supernatural favor upon our lives. Did I hear someone say "Favor aint fair"... oh yes it is!!! He decided to favor you and I! It's all good!

Try again. Fill in the blank: "Because He is_____ I am
_____
_____
_____.

God gave us each a duty. Notice I said duty not job. A job is a piece of work, one that is paid for an agreeable price. A duty is an obligation! We did not negotiate or convene with God about our role in the earth. He assigned us each the duty to be fruitful, to multiply and subdue the earth. Each of us was created with the seed we need to feed! We are equipped with the supply necessary to reproduce, cultivate and subjugate (conquer) in the earth! Please don't be discouraged by the false image of failure or delay. God has a good plan for your life according to Jeremiah 29:11 and there is provision for the vision. Just as he supplied the plant and the trees to yield fruit with seed, so it shall be with us! There is provision for the vision. It takes time to bear fruit but thank God we have the seed! It shall produce and yield its harvest in due season!

Genesis 18:14 asked a question, "Is there anything too hard for the Lord?" Here the promise. "At the time appointed I will return unto thee, according to the time of life". I encourage you to be watchful for the appointed time of life is now. Your seeds had to "die" in the ground to sprout life; just as the first sign of Spring. New life has now grown into its intended purpose and low hanging fruit is ripening. Oh taste and see that the Lord is good! He promises, if we be willing and obedient, we shall eat the good of the land (Isaiah 1:19). There are two unchangeable things we can depend upon, God's promise and his oath (Hebrews 6:17-20).

What he says, we will see. What we see, he has said! Bless his holy name! He's a good Father.

That's who he is and we are loved by him. That's who we are and were intended to be! Loved by Love!

He saw everything he made was good and pondered it is good, and good indeed! He said, "Let us make man in our image". The question is, is what he saw different than what he said? No! In order for him to see what he saw (which was good) what he said had to first be good. He himself FIRST was GOOD!!! Hallelujah! God is good all the time and all the time God is good! Thank you Lord! What he has spoken for your life is incomprehensible!

Practice makes perfect. Fill in the blank: "Because He is_____ I am _____and it is _____.

Psalms 100: 5 says "For the Lord is good; his mercy is everlasting; and his truth endures to all generations."!! Oh yes it's true, HE is good and so is everything else! Everything about you is good. Everything connected to you is good. Everything that shall come from you shall be good! Believe it today! The Lord saw you before conception, and knew you before the womb and what he SEEN WAS GOOD!!!

Joy Overall Is Yours!

5 To Be Rich

When you receive it, you'll receive it!

(Mark 11:24)

Do you remember that 80's song by Calloway "I Wanna Be Rich"? Very catchy, great hook! The lyrics "I want money, lots and lots of money; I want the pie in the sky. ...I wanna be rich". If you are like me, an old song comes to mind before you know it, you're singing the tune. That is exactly what happened to me except I changed the lyrics! Ready On the Mic: **REMIX**!!!!!!!

"I want favor, lots and lots of favor, I want abundant life for your glory, only for your glory, be pleasing in your sight

I'm blessed to be RICH! oh-oh-oh I'm blessed to be Rich"...

(THANKS FOR SINGING ALONG!)

The story of the Rich Fool in Luke 12: 13-21 begins with a man who covets his brother's share of an inheritance; requesting that he be made to share it with him. The Lord first responds with a word of rebuke cautioning such sin, expressing a man's life does not consist in the abundance of possessions. He continues with a parable of a rich man who produces a plentiful crop. Rather than the rich man sharing of his abundance with others, **he hoards his harvest,** at which his life is required.

Remember the crop is "Harvested to Help."

There are two characters:

1. **The Coveter**- feeling strong or immoderate desire for that which belongs to someone else, who has the intense wishing and longing for something of another's.

The bible speaks clearly against coveting. God has no respect of person, and he is a God of plenty. He is the Father in heaven who gives good gifts to those who ask him (Matt 7:11). What he has done for one he is able to do for another. He is not short of supply of anything. Be confident in the fact that those who seek the Lord lack no good thing (Psalm 34:10). You are exceedingly blessed! You are exceedingly rich! Careful consideration of our own "wealth" deters coveting another's. You are his workmanship and he has made you to be a blessing! Similar to a personal trust fund- access is not granted until maturity is acquired! Praise God for your tailored made Trust Fund. We thank God in advance for unlimited access, withdrawals & interest! We are the kingdoms physical banking institution! You and I are walking ATMS, Banks and Financial investors. We house his glory, we house his riches and we house his wealth.

2. **The Hoarder**- the one who's excessive in acquiring things but has an inability or unwillingness to discard, share or release them.

Acquiring unto yourself, while neglecting the care to be rich in the things of God; herein the offence. He in turn loses everything.

Verse 21.

"So is he that layeth up treasure for himself, and is not **Rich** toward God." (KJV)

"That's what happens when you fill your barn with self and not with God." (MSG)

"So it is for the one who continues to store up and hoard possessions for himself, and is not rich {in his relationship} toward God."(AMP)

There is no injustice in riches or wealth, as a matter of fact God endorses both according to 2 Chronicles 1:12,

Proverbs 10:22 and Deuteronomy 8:18. However as we build, through Christ unto ourselves (horizontally), we must take great concern to build unto Christ (vertically).

2 Corinthians 8:9 (NASB)

For you know the grace of our Lord Jesus Christ, that though He was rich, yet for your sake became poor, so that you through his poverty might become rich.

To be rich in God, rich toward God! Rich in faith. Rich in good works. Rich in grace and mercy. Rich in love and truth. Rich in spiritual gifts. Rich in righteousness!

Literally Christ became poverty that we may live richly, abundantly wealthy. Where then is the breakdown of transference?

1Timonthy 6:17-19 (KJV)

Charge them that are rich in this world, that they be not high minded, nor trust in uncertain riches, but in the living God, who gives to us richly all things to enjoy; that they do good, that they be rich in good works, ready to distribute, willing to communicate (share), laying up for themselves a good foundation against the time to come, that they may lay hold on eternal life.

My former relationship and previous lack of understanding regarding money hindered and prevented my ability to manage it, earn it and supply it. Pride and the concept of being an independent woman nearly destroyed me! The scripture above references uncertain riches. Without thought, I had put my trust in the arms of flesh. I worked multiple jobs, tried the pyramid businesses, and hustled here and there thinking I had to manipulate time and energy to earn wealth. In all my efforts, I was still living paycheck to pay check, robbing Peter to pay Paul, and barely at times affording something to eat. There were two revelations that enlightened my understanding.

The first being, "When you receive it, you will receive it." Our ability to believe directly impacts our ability to receive, according to Mark 11:24. The moment you believe, should be in essence the exact same moment (by faith) you receive it! The scripture said "when" you pray, not after. I had a heart to heart conversation with myself one evening. I told myself, "Shay, until you can put up shut up." I realized that until I was able to put my faith where my mouth was, things weren't going to change. Nothing will change until you are able to believe that which you speak! On the other hand, once I believed, I couldn't stop speaking life into everything I desired! I even woke myself up out of a deep sleep declaring and decreeing! I guess if you're going to talk in your sleep, at least say something worth hearing!

Holy Spirit spoke such a powerful word to me when I was in a financial strain one time. He said, "All that is Mine is thine." With these words came revelation that everything that belongs to the Lord, belongs to me. Because I am one with God, there is no separation between what he has and what I have! Initially I processed the information so narrowly, until Holy Spirit enlightened me that this includes his mind, his attributes, his will and authority. The strain appeared to be financial in the natural, when in actuality the shortage was in wisdom! Upon asking for what I thought I needed, I was given what I had not yet attained; I needed revelation of who I was in Christ and who Christ was in me. I needed sound judgement and wisdom. All I was required to do was receive the wisdom, implement the strategy and the streams of income began to follow.

I am learning and implementing the wealth blueprint from heaven in my life! The revelation changed my relationship and how I view money. The blueprint gave me a plan of action to work toward my financial goals, no matter how long it takes. I had to learn to sow seed from a place of charity and cheer, without fear or worry. This experience taught me to pray from a posture of having already received rather than from a position of begging and pleading. The blessing of the Lord makes me rich and adds no sorrow! My Father is rich, therefore so am I! I am the blessed of the Lord. He has made me a blessing to all the families of the earth according to Genesis 12:2-3, therefore riches and wealth are my portion and inheritance!

With Christ, we are rich! We are joint heirs with Christ in the Kingdom. In everything we are enriched in Him! He has shown us his surpassing riches of grace and kindness unto repentance. He is such a faithful and loving God. I decree by faith, that in all things we are rich as Jesus Christ is rich in all things! I speak that our hearts are encouraged, are knit together in love, attaining all the wealth/riches that come from the full assurance of understanding, true knowledge of Christ himself.

Begin to meditate on that! Let your spirit explore the vastness of your earthly and kingdom possessions!

Declare "All that is Thine is Mine!"

6 WON'T HE DO IT

Won't he do it?

He has already done it!

"O Lord God, You have only begun to show your servant Your greatness and Your mighty hand; for what god is there in heaven or on earth that can do such works and mighty acts (miracles) as Yours? (Deuteronomy 3:24 AMP)

That moment when you are going through the day, taking care of your assigned duties as usual and then something happens. You begin to think of the goodness of Jesus! Without warning all creation pauses and an arousing whirlwind within your spirit overtakes the evident consciousness that you are in public. Time halts with a foreshadowing of praise, and you can't restrain yourself. Everything within you comes into a collaborative agreement to scream a hallelujah, or a thank you Jesus. Maybe you rise from your desk or cubical because your hands and feet conspire to offer an unchoreographed praise dance. Maybe you're watching online or listening during a peaceful time of devotion and it happens...your pupils dilate, your heart beats rapidly and your breath becomes filled with exuberant shout waiting to be released. Maybe you're driving and the mile markers begin to diminish because your tear ducts have begun to swell, releasing tears as rain upon your cheeks similar to a sudden spring shower upon a windshield. There, right then and there, you lose yourself in the presence of God! Your praise merges with the heavenly hosts, and together as one vocal symphony, explodes a concert of praise!

Why? Because of who he is and because of what he has done! That issue, that concern that kept you on your knees, that prayer that you petitioned with fervency, earnest and conviction; that circumstance that was so seemingly impossible, that desire without wavering kept near the fire, that family member that you pinned to the altar of your heart...that need that caused you to say "I've been waiting so long but Lord I trust you", "Lord it's in your hands". That one thing that provoked bravery and fight from deep within. Yes, He did THAT thing!!!! He selected a moment from eternity and placed it in the restraints of time from the beginning of your time for the manifestation of his glory to be revealed. Without coercion, He did it! Won't He do it! It's already done!

MIRACLE

Just as he snatched the Shunammite woman's son from the cold grip of death....she ran with resolve that it had to be well because if anyone could do it, or would do it... It would be him to do it! (2 Kings 4:8-37 KJV)

SIGN

Similar to Moses and the camp, whose backs were being hunted by a barbaric Pharaoh, yet their faces forward an endless sea. He stretched out his hand over the sea and the sea receded as a dividing wall. (Exodus 14:16-22 KJV)

WONDER

Just as Peter shackled, chained and isolated enforced by 16 guards. When no one could get in or out, an angel made himself known, and the gates opened on their own accord, that he should be freed. (Acts 12:1-11 KJV)

IT'S A FINISHED WORK. IT'S ALREADY DONE!

You may be facing tragedy, crisis or calamity as the Shunammite woman. Maybe you have experienced loss. It does not have to be a physical person but it can be a state or condition. There is hope and there is life. We have a high priest that is touched with the feeling of our infirmities (Hebrews 4:15). He cares. He came that we might have life and that more abundantly. Run with resolve into the arms of Christ, with "It Is Well" faith, for he is the giver of life. The spirit of God made you and the breath of life of the almighty he has given you! We declare that everything you breathe upon through prayer and song shall live; health, businesses, family members, ministry, body, ideas, finances etc. LIVE. Come alive NOW in Jesus name. (Job 33:4 KJV)

Feeling like your back is against the wall? You've come too far to turn back but what's ahead seems to present the same risk if not greater? The story of Moses is saturated with examples of trial vs triumph. His challenges were many, however with each challenge God made provision for him to overcome. When food was scarce he fed them manna from heaven. When friends became foes he opened up the earth that they would be swallowed. When he needed guidance and understanding, God invited him to the top of the mountain. When he needed protection, he hide them in a cloud by day and a ring of fire by night! The place he thought he could not pass through became a grave yard for all he had to come through! Won't he do it! The Lord fights for you, you need only be still. He shall provide. (Exodus 14:14). (Psalms 91:7 AMP).

Restricted? Confined? Bound? Captive? Or maybe in a "holding cell/ Holding pattern"...Today is your day of freedom. There is power in the name of Jesus to break every chain! Every yoke, chain, soul tie, unhealthy relationship, generational curse, stronghold of bondage and slavery be broken by the power of the blood of

Jesus! You are free and free indeed. No chains holding you! It was for this freedom that Christ set us free [completely liberating us]; therefore keep standing firm and do not be subject again to a yoke of slavery (Galatians 5:1 AMP). It has been removed. No guard, troop, regime or army can keep you from purposes, plan, provisions and promises of God! For by Christ you can crush a troop, and by your God you can leap over a wall! (Psalm 18:29) Be Free!

WONT HE DO IT!

We serve the God of Moses, Peter and the Shunammite woman! We serve the God that parts seas, raises the dead, causes walls to destruct and fold. Our God is the God of Abraham, Isaac and Jacob. All that he performed on their behalf, he is willing and able to perform on ours as well! Won't he do it!

A Prayer of Declarations: Encouraged

It is true that as we contend for the faith, we at times are in need of encouragement. It was David that said he would have fainted had he not believed to see the goodness of the Lord in the land of the living. As I prayed today, these were the words impressed upon my heart. I pray that as you pray these words you find encouragement and strength.

I decree quantum leaps in the spirit. I decree manifestations of what I have believed by faith. I will finish strong in the strength of God. I will pursue the purposes of God. I will hear and obey, and say what God says. I will do great exploits in the earth. I decree the best days of my life are now and they shall remain. I decree that I shall be named among the remnant, among the true worshippers, among the blessed. I receive the present help of Christ to accomplish all that I set my heart to. I call my thoughts, my words, my relationships, friendships, finances, skills & talents all into order and divine alignment with the will of God for my life. I am not discouraged. I am not forgotten. I am not alone. I am not behind; but I am synchronized with the diving timing of heaven. I walk in abundance in every area of my life. I choose to redefine, reimage, rebrand, repent and restore the assignment upon my life and entire household. I will no longer entertain contrary evidence of any kind. I will no longer strive against the shift or separation. I am who God says that I am. I am chosen. I am loved. I am strong. I am set apart. I am anointed, powerful, and wealthy in all things. I operate in the fullness of God's grace and spirit. I will no longer look to friends, family or any human connection to affirm, endorse or validate me, but I will look to the word of God. I decree all wounds bound and healed. I decree every lie and root of falsehood, uprooted and in its place, truth & life are established. I command surpassing peace, abundant life, fullness of joy, love and multiplied faith to be my counterparts. Wisdom is my kindred and peace is my exactor. I exercise the authority given unto me to rule, reign and reside in the realm of the supernatural. I decree the old man is dead and the new man is alive, consumed with the fire of God. Now I am ready. I am ready to receive visions, dream and prophetic instructions. I am ready to call forth miracles, signs and wonders. I am ready to access new levels, new realms. I am ready to walk through new doors, new portals. I am ready to confront oppositional forces that come to deter me from my destiny. I am ready to stand, even if that stance is without popularity. I am ready to be everything I've always wanted to see. I will. I shall. I am encouraged.

                Joy Overall Is Yours!

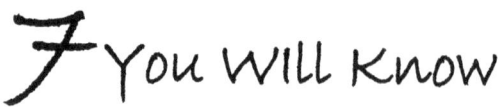 You Will Know

Get wisdom, get life.

"And the Lord answered me, and said, write the vision, and make it plain upon tables, that he may run that readeth it."

Habakkuk 2:2

What do I? When do I? How do I? Where do I?

What do you do when His plan doesn't unfold as you planned? What do you choose when neither option is what you asked for? How do you respond when evil confronts your good? When you prepared for the right lane and the Lord says "left lane", When one year becomes two, the friend becomes a foe, when the unexpected is more likely than the expected? Where do you go when you've been to the lowest and higher seems too high? How do you break the cycle and start anew? When is the timing ever perfect?

WHAT DO YOU DO?

Pity party...not an option....Depression... not an option...Run & hide... not an option... Quit, turn back & give up... NOT AN OPTION! All the aforementioned are direct affronts to the promises of God. Sweet Brown said it best, "Aint nobody got time for that". Do we experience these, at times? Yes. Our most infamous and heroic Old Testament and New Testament leaders were acquainted with suffering and suspicion, being perplexed and persecuted. We read their biographies as archaic manuscripts, but the spirit of their commission and their adversity permeates through tales of valor, vengeance and victory!

Your only option is to conquer! Abundant life! The LIFE promised to you! Set your face as a flint. A flint is a hard rock that is able to endure or stand strong against the hard edges of steel, stone and opposition!

Now is not the time to lose discipline, lose momentum, lose ground or lose hope. You are too close! Faith over foolishness!

Why do we perish? We perish for a lack of Knowledge. I decree, not this time. All things purposed and perfect concerning you shall take root deeply to sprout upward and flourish lavishly, more abundantly; you shall no longer dive but thrive!

When you don't know what to do next or how to move forward, the bible says "if any of you lacks wisdom, let him ask of God who gives to all liberally and without reproach, and it will be given to him" (James 1:5 NKJV).

"Wisdom, like an inheritance, is a good thing; it benefits those who see the light of day. Wisdom provides protection, just as money provides protection. But the advantage of knowledge is this: Wisdom preserves the life of its owner". (Ecc 7:11-12 NET)

Another translation says, "but the excellency of knowledge is, that wisdom gives life to them that have it" (KJV).

This scripture is so good! Read it again. Do you see the concept of inheritance, benefits, light, protection, advantage, preservation and life? Wisdom, knowledge and understanding are so much more than "knowing and the Know how". They are likened to keys that unlock the mysteries, the divine inspiration of the Holy Spirit enlightening us.

Wisdom bestows well-being. Knowledge bestows power. Understanding bestows prudence.

All three are given by the Lord. God gives wisdom freely, is plainspoken in knowledge and understanding. He's an endless surplus of common sense for those who live well, a personal bodyguard to the candid and sincere. He keeps his eye on all who live honestly, and pays special attention to his loyal committed ones (Prov 2:6-8 Msg).

Make a conscious decision with intentionally aligned efforts, that you will reach your expected end. By faith, you will govern all your affairs after wisdom, knowledge and understanding, being now enlightened of such begets LIFE. DEFENCE.INHERITANCE!

Big dreams, big plans equates to big work. There are some who have an illustrated strategy of how they will gracefully arrive at success of their pursuit. Then there are others whose portrait scope is vast but the paint brush has yet to stroke the canvas.

The first few weeks of a new year are propelled with the fuel of impossibilities. The vision is clear, and the imagination broad. We see the current state and future status but what about the middle, where the "know how" lives. You may not have all the details, resources or even the full understanding right now in the natural. Yet, by faith you have all things needed and desired through Christ Jesus to bring his name fame! Understanding of the vision is vitally important as manifesting the vision. In all our efforts to produce, let us remember that there is assistance and insight available to us from God, the Father.

Such was the case with Daniel.

"Yea, while I was speaking in prayer, even the man Gabriel, whom I had seen in the vision at the beginning, being caused to fly swiftly, touched me about the time of the evening sacrifice. And he informed me, and talked with me, and said, O Daniel, I am now come forth to give thee skill (insight) and understanding. At the beginning of thy supplications the commandment came forth, and I am come to shew thee; for thou art greatly beloved: therefore understand the matter, and consider the vision." (Daniel 9:21-23 KJV)

I love this passage. Daniel was praying to the Lord regarding a vision he seen. An angel, Gabriel swiftly came to his aid. Not only did he come but he touched him, informed him and spoke with him directly. He came to give him insight and understanding of what was to come. What I find encouraging was that "at the beginning" of Daniel's prayer, a commandment to assist him was decreed! Wow! At times we feel as though a prayer unanswered, is a prayer unheard; Not So! Every prayer is heard and every prayer in faith is answered! Uncertainty can be a distraction. It was not that the prayer had not been received. The utterance was heard but the answer had to travel through realms and dimensions of opposition and rebuttal.

Gabriel affirmed Daniel and encouraged him to get a full view of the whole matter!

God is ready and able to hear our prayers and to answer them with peace! Those who are acquainted with Jesus Christ are afforded grace for every task and assignment. Let us approach boldly before the throne of grace, being reverent in our communion with him, that he may reveal his mysteries and guide us into his perfect purpose and plan. Know that when we pray up, our heaven Father looks down! He is attentive to our call for assistance in every endeavor, so much so that he commands the angels to keep watch over us and the fulfilment of his will for our lives! He's so awesome.

As you put your hand to the plow for the vision, take comfort in knowing that you have angels that are employed by heaven to aid in your success; ready to touch you, speak with you and inform you of the details of the vision God has given you! Don't worry about the "how", rests in all things are possible to him that believes. Commit your way unto the Lord, commit the vision he's given to you back to him and shall make your way prosperous and your path straight! Go for it! Go for it with joy!

GET WISDOM. GET KNOWLEDGE. GET UNDERSTANDING.GET LIFE!

1. Ask for Wisdom, knowledge and understanding.

2. Believe when you pray you receive.

3. Implement the strategy.

4. Follow instruction.

5. Obey the word.

""Wisdom is of utmost importance, therefore get wisdom, and with all your effort work to acquire understanding". Prov 4:7

"This book shall not depart out of thy mouth; but thou shalt meditate therein day and night, that thou may observe to do according to all that is written therein: for then thou shalt make thy way prosperous, and then thou shalt have good success." I decree and declare that we shall have greater success this year and supernatural advancement in all things we put our hands toward! Go forth, and be fruitful! Thank you Lord for answering prayers!

8 What Do You See?

Abba, I am what you see.

Have you ever looked at an optical illusion? A group of individuals can look at the same picture and see different things? Take a moment to observe the illusion below. **What do you see?**

• •   • • • •

•   •   •

Some may see nine dots. Perhaps initially you see a triangle, a grouping of dots or nothing at all. The illusion challenges not necessarily what you see but what you have the capacity to see. How vast is your imagination? How descriptive are the pages of your mind?

For me, well I see absolutely nothing but a bunch of dots randomly placed in available space on this page, but that's merely because that's exactly what I did!!!!!! I hope I didn't take away from any of your deep analytical design of the dots!!! Hopefully you are laughing now that you know it was a trick!!!

Ok, back to the point! The purpose was to challenge the vastness of your imagination. You can see whatever you choose to see per your point of reference and perspective!

"More over the word of the Lord came unto me, saying, Jeremiah, "What do you see?" And I said, "I see a branch of an almond tree." Then said the Lord to me, "You have seen well: for I am (actively) watching over my word to fulfill it." The word of the Lord came to me a second time, saying, "What do you see?" And I said, "I see a boiling pot, tilting away from the north."{Jeremiah 1:11-15 AMP}.

Let's Look at the vocabulary: *See*

- Perceive with eyes, discern visually, foreseeing, near-sighted.
- View or predict as a possibility.
- Agreement, continued attention (Transliteration)

Hebrew: Raah (See)

- Access, Understand or think, approve, select, search or regard

Why would the Lord ask, "What Do You See? Why would he

It appears that the Lord will show us what we have the capacity to perceive, so that we may conceive! Soon after Jeremiah's response, he was charged to "speak", this was his assignment {1:17}. Look at the vocabulary..."view or predict as a possibility" or "access or understand, with continued regard." We can only see what we can perceive. If the eye hasn't seen it, the heart is unable to conceive it {1 Corinthians 2:9}. I am not talking about temporal sight. I'm speaking of spiritual insight. If we don't look, we won't see, and if we don't see, we won't have anything to speak. Remember he asked "What do you see?" in other words TELL ME WHAT YOU SEE. Jeremiah,

Amos {Amos 8:1-2} and Zechariah {Zech. 4:1-3} were all posed with this exact question. Each of them perceived, spoke and conceived.

When Jeremiah saw rightly, the Lord promised to hasten his word to perform it. Could it be that it is not about what you see, but HOW you see what you see? Are you near sighted or farsighted? How close does a sign of "it shall come to pass" need to be in order for you to SEE it correctly?! We declare 20/20 vision, for you to see the plans and purposes of God for your life (without obstruction) rightly and perfectly, with clarity even if they are invisible, even if in this present time it appears bleak and dim! We believe to see the beauty of holiness as bright cosmic colors bursting forth through the darkness as a rainbow does through the clouds! Remember, we are unlocking the Joy in your journey. No matter what it appears to be, it's what you SEE that shall BE! Take a journey here.

I pose the question to you, **"What do you SEE?"**

I SEE my family whole, reconciled, prospering and in good health. I SEE mothers drawn to the hearts of their daughters and fathers drawn to the hearts of their sons. I SEE the statistic of failed Christian marriages being reversed. I SEE our country returning to God, penitent and humble. I SEE a cure for the epidemic of HIV/AIDS, Cancer and diverse diseases. I SEE African American men having equal access to employment and wrongful convictions vindicated. I SEE wealth, elevation and promotion for me and all those connected to me.

Practice "Seeing", perceiving. Practice "speaking what you see." This is a faith activity. Speak what you see until you see what you've said! Once you **SEE**, **SPEAK** the word over it that you may **CONCEIVE** it, for the Lord said he is actively watching over HIS word to fulfill it!

It is so and it shall be!

What do you see?

_____
_____
_____
_____
_____
_____
_____
_____
_____
_____
_____.

9 Come Thirsty

**If I could drink you in, let it be that I might swim within.
My ocean deep, you have become.**

"For I will pour water upon him that is thirsty, and floods upon the dry ground: I will pour my spirit upon thy seed, and my blessing upon thine offspring." Isaiah 44:3 KJV

I began to meditate on what the Father was speaking to me through this passage, the song "Just Want You" by Travis Greene began to play. My spirit started to swell with a very simple request, "Lord, take everything. I don't want it. I don't need it. I just want you."

You are mine. I am yours. I just want you, all of you. More of you. All that I can drink in. As a tree is known by its fruit, so is a fountain known by its streams. The Lord spoke of a covenant blessing, not water but his spirit to me.

"If any man thirst, let him come unto me, and drink. He that believeth on me, as the scripture hath said, out of his belly shall flow rivers of living water." John 7:38-39

> There are many things that we at times, have used as substitutes to satisfy an inward craving, a desperate longing; the *THIRST*.

Relationships

Sex

Professional Roles

Family

Monetary Gain

Violence

Approval Seeking

Possessions

Friendships

Alcohol

Public Reputation

Status

Caregiving

Drugs

Titles

Academic Achievement

Materialism

Food

Extreme Risk Taking

Cosmetic Surgery

Success

All of which have the capability to become idols, but incapable of being God.

"To whom will you liken me, and make me equal, and compare me, that we may be alike?"

"Remember the former things of old: for I am God, and there is none else; I am God, and there is none like me."

None of which are capable of quenching our thirst with living water! Living, because his spirit, his presence is as water. It's motion. It's life. It's healing. Nothing can satiate the thirst except the love of God. He created us with an innate trigger of dependency upon him, and him alone (Isaiah 46:3-4 KJV).

In all our searching, and sometimes artificial replacements, there is nothing that will satisfy our souls like the rivers of living water, his spirit. The Samaritan woman at the well, came thirsty. She drank and received everlasting life (John 4:7-26).

He will pour out on ground, on the heart that is thirsty. They that hunger and thirst after righteousness shall be filled (Matt. 5:6).

All who are thirsty, come and drink. Drink from the spiritual Rock, Jesus Christ (I Cor. 10:4). In some foreign countries, they kneel at the river and drink with their hands, others come bearing a pitcher or bucket to draw water with. It is not what you draw with but how you come. Come thirsty. When we come to "draw" from him, he is ready and willing to pour! His well runs deep and never runs dry.

Thirsty? Drought season? Dry? There is a fountain that flows from Immanuel's veins. These waters flow to every valley, mountain and desert place in your life. No boundary or geographical limitation. Where you are, his spirit is also if you will drink. Drink from the well that won't run dry. This well of living water, is a fountain sprout that restores, cleanses and makes whole. The spiritual drink of the Rock empowers, redeems and recovers!

"When the poor and needy seek water, and there is none, and their tongue fails for thirst, I the Lord will hear them, I the God of Israel will not forsake them. I will open rivers in high places and fountains in the valleys: I will make the wilderness a pool of water and the dry land springs of water (Isaiah 41:17-18).

On average the body can survive 3 days without water, maximum recorded is between 8-10. How long would your spirit survive without the "living water"?

10 Customized Blessing

One size does not fit all, that's why we have options!

Something big is on the horizon! I was driving and two words leaped in my spirit, Customized Blessing!

A Customized Blessing means that whatever he has designed for you is fitted to suit just YOU! One size does not fit all. The master seamstress, the master tailor creatively fashioned each of us with preferences, specifications and measurements that encompass the width, length, height or depth of who we are individually, that are separate from any other "similar design". Your blessing is not like anybody else's because it's yours, sown for you to own! It has your name written all over it! There's nothing like a tailored made suit! All things considered for the "runway".

Customized: Only one of its kind, made with a specific person in mind!

King David came to mind first, how Saul "gifted" him his armor to fight against Goliath, but it did not prove to profit him any because although it was fashioned for purpose it was fitted for another person. (1 Samuel 17:38:39 KJV)

King Solomon came to mind next. The Lord said to him, "What do you want from me (MSG)? Or another interpretation says he instructed him "Ask what I shall give thee". 2 Samuel 12:7-8 (KJV). Solomon proceeds to recognize the covenant between God, his Father David and the favor he has been given as King. He proceeds to ask God for **three things**; yet these "simple" three things are customized with provision, tailored to perfection and fitted for generational blessings! I am convinced that Solomon had no idea what he had "really" asked for.

Solomon's 3 requests were:

1. Let the WORDS (promises) you spoke to my father be established {even now, for you have made me King}

This request was genius! He asked God to honor an aforementioned promise, that he himself was not a witness to, but his Father was! What has God promised your mother or father, that you now have rights to claim? There are ancient mantles, dowries and gifts left behind by your ancestors that you can now state claim to!

According to 2 Samuel 7:12-17 the promises were-

a. His Kingdom be established

b. A house built for the Lord's name

c. The throne of his Kingdom established forever

d. God takes the parental role as "Father" or "Lordship"

e. The descendent takes the role of "Sonship"

f. Mercy will never depart from him

(ONE REQUEST INCLUDED 7 BLESSINGS)

2. **WISDOM**- the quality of having experience, knowledge, good judgment.

Such humility exemplified. He asks God for an understanding heart to judge his people fairly, being able to discern (perceive or recognize) between what is good and what is evil. (1 King 3:9 KJV)

According to Proverbs 4: 6-7 with wisdom comes-

a. Protection

b. Preservation

c. Treasures (Colossians 2:2-3)

d. Purity, Peace, Gentleness, Easy to be entreated (appeal to), Merciful with good fruit and without partiality or hypocrisy (James 3:17 KJV)

e. Blessing & Happiness (Prov 3:13)

f. Increase in learning (Prov 1:5)

g. Strength (Prov 24:5)

(ONE IS MULTIPLIED TO 14 and that's not all)

3. **Knowledge-** information, skills, education, practical understanding, awareness.

A genuine desire to "do it the right way". He asks the Lord for facts & truths, insight & foresight regarding the principles of his role as King and the people he will serve.

According to Proverbs 3: with knowledge comes-

a. Long life

b. Peace

c. Favor

d. Riches & Honor

e. Safety without Stumbling

(ONE IS MULTIPLIED TO 6 and that's not all!)

It might have appeared to you at first that what Solomon asked for was very little, but look at the unobvious, unapparent inheritance he received. His blessings were specific to his purpose, making him like no other King mentioned in the bible! His requests were distinctively allied with his role of leadership and Father incorporated in the granting of three, at least 27 additional provisional blessings! Our God multiplies, he adds, he increases and he enlarges! Little becomes much in the hands of God. Nothing you ask for is proportional to the mighty power of God! He told David "if that had not been enough, I would have given you moreover such and such things (2 Sam. 12:8). The earth is the Lord's and the fullness thereof! Thank you Jesus, we are full!

Just as God customized the blessing for Solomon, and Solomon knew not all that he would be given at his request, God has customized blessings just for you! He has a history of doing just that. He has a proven track record of doing exceedingly and abundantly above all that we could and do ask or think!

You may think that what you have asked for is small and yes it is. It is a small thing for the maker of all things; however this is not the case of "what you see is what you get." No, you are obtaining, attaining, reclaiming, receiving so much more! It's bigger than big! It's better than your best! The next "big" thing in your life is going to BLOW YOUR MIND!

I speak a release of customized blessings in every area of your life! You have asked God for what you thought was "BIG" and he's doing that very thing BIGGER! You have given God a list of "things" and he is saying "You've asked me for many things, but I'm adding all things! My God, this customized blessing is suited with favor and booted with purpose, it's going to be snatchin' and catchin'. Yes I said it! It's going to literally catch some of your enemies by surprise and snatch the attention of those who are looking for the blessed ones of the King of Kings! Your blessings are a witness and testimony, a sign that you are The Blessed! Get happy about it! Rejoice and may your joy run over with confidence that this one is for YOU! You got next!

You need PROOF: Read Malachi 3:12, Isaiah 61:9, Deut 28:10

I thank God that we have examples in the word of God of Customized Blessings! Each never replicated or duplicated!

1. Abraham- Seed was as the sand (Genesis 22:14-16, Genesis 13:14-18)

2. Naaman- Dipped seven times and was made whole (2 Kings 5:10)

3. Leah- Had 6 sons, some of which became descendants of the 12 tribes of Israel (Genesis Chapter 29-30) THANKS LEAH!

4. Simeon- He couldn't die until he seen the Christ (Luke 2:25-32)

5. The Blind man- healed by spit & clay (John 9:1-11)

6. Esther- the orphan who became Queen (the book of Esther)

Just like those mentioned above, you too are receiving a customized blessing! You've asked God for debt cancellation and watch wealth accompany it! You asked God for the city, watch the nation accompany it! You've asked God for help, watch help & Help's helpers accompany it! You've asked him for the one; watch the 100's accompany it!

I BELIEVE GOD! It's going to be exceedingly, abundantly above, that which you have thought, spoken or hoped for in Jesus name! You've asked for the moon, but how do you make room for the universe? You don't, you let God take care of that!!!!

11 You've Been Set Up

All that is well ends well.

I'm sure you can reflect on that exact moment in time where the testing was being built into a testimony. The exact moment the test became a triumph!

Testimony: I am His Worshipper

Despite struggling with my confidence as a result of painful experiences as an adolescent, singing has always been my love language. My childhood church was filled with a family of phenomenal singers. Early on, the choir director identified my gift to sing and would often give me opportunities to lead a solo or a song in the choir. Although there were encouragers who believed in me, their sentiments were pushed into the shadows as the demeaning and critical treatment by others took center stage. These were the beginning roots of rejection, lack of confidence and powerlessness seeded in the soil of my spirit. I felt as though I wasn't good enough and that nothing I did was right. It was impossible to please them.

We were a poor family, accustomed to street life and sin yet a deeply abounding love for people. We didn't have much family and the family we had weren't close, so we looked to the church for love and acceptance. Even in that, Satan would use those closest to me, whom you would think to trust to destroy the hope of my destiny. My mother did her best attempting to shield us from the woes of life as children, yet the undercurrent waves sometimes hit the hardest. We were blessed to be accepted and loved dearly by an amazing core group of members of the church, a couple whom now are the Pastor and First Lady! Without God and their love, we probably wouldn't have made it.

They continuously encouraged me to sing, even when I would cry through an entire solo! I loved to sing. Singing for me was a lifeline. It was like breath. I couldn't casually sing. Every verse, lyric and note of a song would reach to the depths of my soul that I would often weep in awe of God. I was so sensitive and vulnerable to the messages. I didn't know at the time that God had anointed me with a Levitical mantle of worship. We are often inspired to praise and encouraged to worship in our congregational services, but back then no one really taught on what a Worshipper was. What were the biblical standards of a worshipper's character? Or what the burden of this mantle entailed. It was prominently evident that I was an anomaly. The spiritual warfare was intense until I adopted the concept years later "why war when you can worship."

A friend of mine had invited me over for dinner. While standing in her kitchen, she noticed a lump on my neck and asked had that always been that way and was it normal. Prior her to mentioning, I had never noticed. Months later I went to the doctor for a routine annual checkup and he identified multiple lumps in my throat. He scheduled me for a biopsy later that week.

The biopsy results came back malignant goiters; thyroid cancer. I would endure two surgeries for total thyroid removal and cancer treatment as a preventative. The surgeries and radiation left me mute and vocally impaired for nearly a year. For months much of my communication was either by sign, handwriting or a faint whisper, but still no ability to sing. I had been a singer since the age of 2 years old, my mother said. She told me one time I was dancing in front of the TV watching Michael Jackson, and I looked at her and said "One day I'm going to be like him and make you rich". I am still working on that promise!!!

My surgeon scheduled a consultation with me and proceeded to expound in great length that I would never sing again. "If you ever sing again, it will be a miracle." He described the course of the cancer and the intrusive nature of the surgeries as unmerciful. With some reservation, although he was a Christian, he grabbed my hands and began to pray that I would be completely restored. I left him with a whisper, "the next time you see me, I'm going to sing for you." Some time had passed and every day I would test to see the strength of my voice and whether or not I could sing. It seemed as though everyday was a no. Some days I could whisper then other days completely mute. The silence at times would be so overwhelming I until I yielded to the process and began to appreciate the whisper and the audible silence of God's voice.

That may seem strange, but the silence of God has sound. It is as if he's in the room, walking beside you, breathing over and about you but not speaking. It was during this season that I learned to listen intently for his whisper, his song and his instructions. It was in this season that I learned to locate him when I couldn't lean into him. It was in this season that the Lord began to birth the gift of prophecy and prophetic worship in my life. He refined my spiritual eyesight and hearing so profoundly that I would spend upwards of eight hours a day at times listening and meditating, studying the word and worshipping, all in silence. During this season the Lord began to heal the "wounded worshipper" in me and began restoring the love of song. There were nights that I would wake up to an angel of the Lord singing over me and I would listen and write the songs of heaven in a journal. There were days when I would hear a heavenly choir singing all day long, like a radio station of soft classical, mystical instrumentals.

Arriving at a pinnacle point of peace, subdued by angelic minstrels on a clear afternoon something special happened! I was walking around my living room praying mutely. Music was playing in the background, my spirit connected lifted yet at rest. I was moving my lips, silently singing along and the music moved me so emphatically that without contemplation I sang "Hallelujah." A sustained high pitch soprano note sprang up from the oceans floor of my hearts belly, out of the pre and post-surgical hills of my vocal folds, through the creases and folds of my lips like a river flowing, came forth a song! The tone was beautiful, rich and filled with fire! Jubilation within my heart exploded like fireworks on the fourth of July! I stated calling everyone I knew and attempting to sing for them. I called my Pastor and gave him a "leap of faith" date of when I would be returning as the worship leader.

My voice was completely new and so was my confidence. The oil of God upon my life to worship was beyond anything I had ever experienced. A few months passed and the Doctor called me directly and asked that I visit him at the office for my last consultation appointment. My speaking voice was nearly at full capacity, however significantly deeper. As I waited patiently to be seen, I began to worship. The doctor entered and hands raised I was worshipping God singing...

"You are holy, oh so holy.

What a privilege and an honor
To worship at your throne
To be called into your presence
As your own....."
(by Lisa McClendon)

The doctor began to cry. God made me a sign. He made me a miracle. He made me a worshipper! On that very day I vowed to sing to him as he had sang over me all those months. I committed to sing for him as the heavenly hosts are assigned, to worship him from everlasting to everlasting. I vowed to honor him and give him my absolute best, withholding nothing in his presence. He became my audience and serenading him was my sole purpose and my souls delight. It is my innate joy to sing unto the Lord a new song. From that day until now, I am his Worshipper and I worship with Joy! With this sentiment, I took a leap of faith to record my first single!

Take a pause and worship here in this very moment, will you. He is so worthy! Allow the worshipper in you to release a sound that even the angels cannot sing! You can worship from the place of being ransomed and redeemed! What a mighty God we serve! What the enemy meant for bad, God used it for my good. It was a complete set up!

It was a set up for his glory. The test appeared as a setback but it was an opportunity to triumph and for a miracle: Know that the Lord does not have to use unfortunate events to warrant glory. He is glorious!

Sickness becomes health   Poverty becomes wealth   Weakness becomes strength   Curses become blessings...***how it all works together for good to them that love God, to them who are the called according to his purpose. (Romans 8:28 KJV)***

The Lord possessed me in the beginning of his way, before his works of old. I was set up from everlasting, from the beginning, or ever the earth was". (Proverbs 8:22-23 KJV)

Before you and I were formed in the womb, before the night chased after the daylight, before the heavens were prepared and rain fell upon the oceans, both you and I were set up for an eternity. And not just set up, but possessed. Like an orphan adopted! Once separated but grafted into an inheritance of kingdom class! We are of the God class. Heirs, royalty, a child of the King!

The unexpected lay off, God is able to restore and multiply your fruit. The negative Dr. report, God is a healer and makes all things new. The delayed manifestation of a dream or a promise, God is not a man that he she should lie, neither the son of man that he should repent. If he said it, shall he not do it? If he spoke it, he will make it good! (Number 23:19).

You may be hard pressed on every side, but you are not crushed; perplexed but not in despair; persecuted but not abandoned, struck down but not destroyed (2 Cor. 4:8-12) because you are blessed and not cursed. Every one of his promises shall endure. They are yes and amen!

Everything is working together for your good. You shall reap the harvest. The opposition that is preventing you is going to be used to promote you. The test is the bridge to your triumph, you already have the victory! Whatever has been used to block you will be overturned to bless you. (Ezekiel 21:27)

You've been set up for a come up! Read Deuteronomy 28:1-15 for the outlined set up package.

12 Belief For Your Unbelief

Believe Again.

It is possible to have strong faith in one area and weak faith in another. Strong belief in any capacity is attainable in any potentiality.

Mark 9:14-27 tells a story of a scribe's son who was tormented by a violent spirit; one that would resemble what we might call today seizures or convulsions to the most extreme degree. The father is speaking of his son's condition to the disciples in order that they may help but who are unable. The child is brought to Jesus and immediately begins convulsing in his presence. Jesus asks the father, "How long is it ago since this came unto him?' and the father replied "of a child, if you can do anything have compassion on us and help us." Jesus said "If thou can believe, all things are possible to him that believeth". The father cried out with tears, "Lord I believe, help my unbelief. (KJV reference/paraphrase)

Let's look at the vocabulary:

- **Scribe**- acted as the secretary of state, prepared and issued decrees in the name of the King, men of high authority and influence in the affairs of the/a state. Predominantly Levites. Writers. Duplicated and provided instruction of the law. *root meaning*: to set in order.
- **Came** (in this context)- take or occupy a specified position, order or priority.

The role of the scribe from a spiritual perspective: It appears that he has the power to decree a thing and it be established (for his underwriter is the King of Kings), it appears that he has the authority in the Kingdom to influence his affairs and the affairs of others. Not only does he knows the law but also teaches it. He has the capacity to set in order, that which is out of order according to the law of the Kingdom! Such are we, our tongues being as power tools of life and death, creation and formation.

Came is past tense of "come". In order for anything to "Come" it must-

a. Be sent

b. Be invited

c. Have a constructed space or place of destination

Looking at the three above, how might unbelief come?

a. Satan

b. Sin

c. Soul/Relationships

The violent spirit "Came" unto him. It occupied a space within him. Just because something "comes" does not mean it has to "occupy". Unbelief may come but you don't have to allow it to stay. You have the power to decree and demonstrate the word of God over everything pertaining to your life.

The disciples were equipped with power but not prepared for demonstration. The Father was equipped with the Law of the letter but not the legality of authority. He was positioned without possession all due to unbelief.

It is obvious that the Father had some belief, because he asked Jesus for help. So where was the unbelief? I could suggest that he believed Jesus could but doubted if he would. You may have had a similar encounter where you believe in the ability of God (his deity) but not God's ability in you (his divinity).

Have you ever been convinced that he is able for others but considered him absent concerning you? Yes, this is a lie from the pit of hell. God almighty is never absent and he never fails! He knows where you are strong, and I chose to trade weakness for strength! For the bible says "let the weak say they are strong". God said it and that settles it!

Unbelief ties the hand of the Omnipotent and stops the current of favor. Just as a door is an entry for some and an exit for others; our belief (faith) determines whether Jesus, the Lord is a sanctuary or stumbling stone (Luke 2:34-35). Unbelief bars the door. Nothing can get in and nothing can get out. Your prayers don't make it in (up) and his favor doesn't make it out (down).

"And he could do no mighty work, save that he laid his hands upon a few sick folk and healed them. And he marveled because of their unbelief." (Mark 6: 5-6 KJV paraphrased).

Oh the mighty work God desires to do in our lives, if we would just believe. Thank God for his mercy that he is able to help our unbelief by the grace of Holy Spirit.

Jesus asked such a pivotal question. How long since this came unto him?

How long has it been since sorrow and sighing has held your joy captive? When did fear take pre-eminence over your faith? How long has panic stolen the tranquility of your peace? When did it come upon you? You were running well, who did hinder you? Who have you allowed to deter, distract and discourage you?

Is there any unbelief in any area of your life?

Did you know that unbelief grieves the Holy Spirit? (Hebrews 3:18)

Today is the day to renounce double mindedness, doubt and unbelief with fasting and praying. Exercise your legal authority and right to be free from bondage, suspicion, wavering and unbelief. Just as the spirit "came" upon the scribe's son, Jesus lifted him up and he rose. He lifted him from a state of convulsion that left him appearing lifeless and torn. Jesus is able to lift you, restore you, revive you, and re-establish you. Jesus is going to lift you up if you would only believe!

The scripture said Jesus took the young man's hand. I pray that as you read this chapter that you confess and repent of any unbelief, that you begin to express your faith through a demonstration of works, praise and thanksgiving believing that God is not "going to do" but that "he already has" healed you. He has made the way in the wilderness. He has provided pools in the desert place. He has made you glad and your heart to rejoice! I pray that he's visiting you right now. In the presence of the Lord is the fullness of joy and at his right hand pleasures forever more. May the manifested presence of his hand reach to you; grip the palm of your hand. In Jesus mighty name, that there be a lifting now. Your countenance be lifted, your spirit be lifted, your head be lifted, the burdens lifted NOW! You are able to take your own hand, lay it on yourself, be healed and recover your own self if you believe!

You are rising in the power of His word and in the power of your Faith! You are going to believe for all things, hope for all things and trust God through all things, giving him thanks IN all things! I believe for your health, wealth and uncommon favor! Will you today trade any unbelief for belief today? Will you be bold and believe for the "impossible being made possible"?

For we have not received the spirit of bondage again to fear... (Romans 8:15)

God has not given us the spirit of fear, but of power, and of love, and of a sound mind.... (2 Timothy 1:7)

BELIEVE AGAIN.

Belief Qualifications:

1. Believe that HE IS- he exists

Hebrews 11:6 - But without faith it is impossible to please Him; for he that cometh to God must believe that He is, and that he is a rewarder of them that diligently seek him.

2. Work Your Faith- work the word

James 2:14-26- Faith without works is dead. Show your faith by your works.

3. Speak it- Frame your world with your words

Romans 4:17- ...Speaking those things that are not as though they were.

ASSIGNMENT: Write 3-5 faith confessions/belief statements that you are willing to believe and confess for one week. Journal your experience and the results.

1._____
_____

2._____
_____
_____

3._____
_____
_____

4._____
_____

5._____
_____
_____

13 Just a Lil Talk with Jesus

A privileged audience of one will always oblige the empty seats of many others.

"Holy Spirit, this is your blog not mine. What do you want me to write tonight?" I sat still, quietly awaiting a whisper, a still small voice to rise from the silence.

In the distance emerged the words:

"If you were sitting on a bus next to Jesus, what would you talk to him about?"

I would talk to Jesus about Jesus!

I would started by telling him THANK YOU! Thank you Jesus for becoming the sacrifice and the sin offering. Thank you for dying, rising and living that we might have an inheritance of eternal life and salvation. I would thank him for enduring the scoffers, the mockers, the villain's and the betrayer's so that we could have victory over the same characters. I would thank him for being mindful of mankind, enough that we would be created in his image and likeness. I would thank him for mercy, grace and his unfailing love and compassion.

Then I would tell him how much I love him, adore him, have longed to behold him in the beauty of his righteousness. I would speak of his splendor and glory. I would stroke his face with my hands and sing a sweet melody in his ear. I would intimately and affectionately lavish him with my love. I would remove myself from my seat to bow at his feet." I would sit and listen.

Before I knew it, there I was having a full conversation with Jesus, about Jesus! When you talk to Jesus about Jesus, Jesus will talk to you about you...and others too!

He responded:

If only you knew.....

You were created in my God-likeness and image

You are the apple of my eye

You are royalty, a royal priesthood

You are beautiful, fearfully and wonderfully made

You are above only and never beneath

You are never a failure or disappointment

You were created to win and victory is your reward

You are a son of God

You are approved, endorsed, validated and confirmed by God

You are called, chosen, anointed and appointed by God

You are mine and I AM is yours

You are authorized to dominate and reign as a ruler of this land

You are fearless

You are loved, valued and a gift to the kingdom

You are gifted

You are not forsaken, forgotten or tolerated

You are forgiven, preferred and predestined

>If only you knew that all you need is in me. I LOVE YOU.
>
>Beloved, you are my desire and I love you. No toil or tarry, I love you and willing to cover and heal every wound and burden you carry. My eyes are like fire, not to harm, but you my child I chase after to hold in my arms.
>
>Who knows you better than I, of what makes you giggle, laugh smile, no man on earth, every night as you sleep I stay more than a little while to make sure you suffer no hurt.
>
>I wait for you to say good morning, I wait for you to say what's truly in your heart, although every fiber of your being belongs to me, there has always been something about you from the beginning, something special I placed in you from the start.
>
>If only you knew how deeply I love thee, you would never again ponder, "Did he really choose me."
>
>-Pages of my Journal

Jesus said in reference to Mary who "chose that good part, which shall not be taken away from her" (Luke 10:42), she chose an audience with Him! No better audience than an audience of one, with the Son of Man.

We always have audience with Holy Spirit. Not only is he omnipresent but he is eternally existing. He is always there. There is nothing that can separate us from his love neither any geographical location we can hide from his presence. Just the very thought of some sins I've committed, with the lack of regard that God the Father was watching me the entire time makes my eyes cross! What about the "cloud of witnesses"... my goodness... oh Lord, not the angels... Everybody saw that Lord? Funny, not funny!

Oh the mercy and grace he has bestowed upon us. Often we journey in this life as if we are traveling in the shadows, unnoticed without print or identification. He knows us by name and the very number of hairs on our head. Such an intimate God would take interest in such intimate details!

1 Corinthians 2: 7-16.

Acts 13:27

The wisdom of God was not known by the princes of this world, for had they known they would not have crucified the Lord of Glory. Had they known that he was the Messiah, the hope of glory, they would not have moved to condemn him despite not being able to convict him. Had they known that he was the savior and their salvation, they would have spared him. If only they knew that he came to save and not to condemn. He came because of love, to offer salvation. If only they knew.

Verse 9: But as it is written, eye hath not seen, nor ear heard, neither have entered in to the heart of man, the things which God hath prepared for them that love him (is a popular quoted text), but I find inspiration in verse 10-12.

"But God hath revealed them unto us by his spirit: for the spirit searcheth all things, yea the deep things of God. For what man knoweth the things of a man save the spirit of man which is in him? Even so the things of God knoweth no man, but the spirit of God. Now we have received, not the spirit of the world, but the spirit which is of God; that we might KNOW the things that are freely given to us of God." KJV

To know God, is to know his word. To know his word is to know him! He wants us to know him and the things he has prepared for those who love him. He wants us to know the things that are freely given to us of God. They are revealed to us by his spirit.

Above all else, the Father wants us to know that we are loved, accepted and adopted by him. We don't have to search, inquire or pursue the love of another. He emptied heaven of its most valuable possession and would trade earth for you and I. He would again die, just for one in order that no child be left behind. He gave his best and he gave his all. How precious is the unfailing, never ending, overwhelming love of God! To them that call upon his name he is abounding and always in their midst, rejoices over us with gladness. We have a place of belonging, a place of safety and security within the love of Jesus. In him is truly the awe of love!

If only you knew the hope of his calling, the depth of his love, the weight of his glory, his gift of life everlasting. If only you knew the broadness of his shoulders to bare the weight of your burdens, if only you knew the strength of his arms to carry you through every storm, if only you knew the sound of his voice that calls you by name. Just a lil talk with Jesus makes it right!

Scripture of Meditation: Ephesians 1:18--23.

Practice being in his presence!

14 BE GREAT

The greatness of a woman is not how tall she stands, but how tall she allows God to stand within her.

There is something great that you are to manifest in the earth. You have a dream, a purpose and passion burning within you to do something extraordinary. Might I remind you that you are chosen for greatness! God promises that greater works shall we do!

"Verily truly I tell you, whoever believes in me will do the works I have been doing, and they will do even greater things than these, because I am going to the Father.'"
(John 14:12 NIV).

What is that awesome, creative idea you are "withholding" and why? Is it fear, does the dream "appear" bigger than you? Could it be past failed attempts/fear of failure? Is it resources? Maybe you feel you are not equipped or somebody else could do it better?

Whatever the case may be, the Lord chose you to accomplish it! He has equipped and provided all things necessary (according to faith and the power that works in us!) for your success!

The spirit spoke this:

"Be wise; let not your admiration of someone else's dream be the assassination of your own."

Everyone these days seems to be "winning", "working on something", "living on purpose"...and if you are not careful to remain focused on your dream; your season of "preparation" will become convoluted by your perceived success of others and impede your ability to produce. There is a set time for everything. You have conceived the dream now focus on perpetuating the outcome of it! Look within not without! It's that time to shift from "What about me Lord?" To "We got this Jesus!"

Manifestation is NOW, with the supernatural speed and breath of God. He has confirmed you. He has endorsed you. He has validated you and yes it was he that gave you that dream; that revelation! Instead of "standing with God"... Go and Flow with God!!! There's a spiritual acceleration available to you. Rise up believing in who God says you are and what God says you WILL do!

"You'll take delight in God, the Mighty One, and look to him joyfully, boldly. You'll pray to him and he'll listen; he'll help you do what you've promised. You'll decide what you want and it will happen; your life will be bathed in light. To those who feel low you'll say, chin up! Be brave! Job22:26-29

(Malachi 3:11 & 1 Thess 5:24 references)

Be encouraged! It will happen! Focus on allowing your dream to live!

Imagine it. What does it look like? I often ask the question if you were afforded the opportunity to live your dream or "best life" within the blink of an eye, what that life looks like. Rarely is someone able to tell me. If they do answer, the adjectives of their announced "best life" are often vague, ambiguous and dated for an offset retirement. Our future is now!

In order for the dream to live it first has to be given life! How does that happen?

Conceptualization + Imagination + Formulation

= Actualization.

Idea/Thought + Picture/ Image + Work/ Plan

= Manifestation

Let's look at some vocabulary:

Imagination-the faculty or action of forming new ideas, or images or concepts of external objects not present to the senses. To form a mental image or picture of something not in yet physical form (abstract image). To give an image/form/illustration to something without form. You have to see it in order to see it! According to your faith, be it unto you! Matthew 9:29

Conceptualization- the action or process of forming a concept or thought of something (abstract idea). It's a derivative of the word concept (a thought or idea conceived in the mind) from the Latin term "conceptus" or "concipere" which means to take in, conceive or receive! In other words, if you can conceive it in the womb of your mind, you can receive it in the palm of your hand! Hebrews 11:11

Formulation- the action of devising or creating something, the development or preparation of a plan, structure or system, a putting together of methods, components according to a formula. Here you have what I suggest to be the "action fraction". Faith without works is dead! James 2:20

Now your time to shine has arrived and there's a sense of intimidation in the spotlight.

I've heard many say, I'm comfortable with being in the background, I don't like a lot of attention etc. all that is fine, but what if your destiny demands that your name be made great? What if your destiny demands that you forfeit being reclusive and step into the spotlight? Of course not for your own glory, but that men would see your good works and glorify the Father which is in heaven. What if the very light you are hiding under a bushel is the same light that is to attract and provoke the light of greatness in others?

The scripture Joshua 1:5 came to mind..."No one will be able to stand against you all the days of your life. As I was with Moses, so I will be with you; I will never leave you nor forsake you.

For years Joshua followed Moses, witnessing all of his great exploits, seeing the favor of God upon his life. He was a student of greatness. He was maturing, while learning to master the art of leadership. His time in discipleship, as a follower, the time in the shadows was serving a greater purpose; not to hide him but to cover him while he was being cultivated. Joshua didn't become great at the time of his appointment. Joshua, all along during his tutelage under Moses, was indeed and had always been GREAT! The syncopated timing and assignment had finally come into alignment!

Genesis 12:2 "I will make your name great."

His time had come. It was Joshua's divine time to shine! The Lord reassured him that just as he was Lord of miracles for Moses, so would he be the Lord of miracles and great exploits for him.

You were born to be great and do great things in the earth. You may have felt like the underdog, the last or the least, but all along you've been engrafted with a seed of greatness! Everything you need has always been on the inside of you! Greater works shall you do, said Jesus to his disciples, not as a suggestion but rather as a seal and indoctrination of approval to do the greater work. Jesus, himself came in such lowly form in the garments of a servant with the purpose of being our savior.

Do you struggle with acknowledging and accepting the greatness within? Why?

Could the conflict be that it is difficult to identify with your greatness within because you identify more with the "garments of your flesh" than you do with the purpose of your spirit?

Paul said I glory in my infirmities! He is one of our notable examples of a man rude in speech, frail in stature, of corrupted reputation but wealthy in knowledge, without limited power and a converted spirit of incorruptible seed, his accomplishments without dispute! He knew he had issues, but those issues were lame and made impotent by the hand of God upon his life! The hand of God is upon your life and nothing you encounter or assume to be lacking in resource, character or opportunity diminishes that.

Whomever he equips he also called! You are the total package! Nothing more, nothing less! In Christ you are complete! Go be great in the earth!

Apologize no longer! Do not apologize for being great! Do not apologize for being chosen! Do not apologize to compensate for others misunderstanding your greatness. Not everyone will get it or get you!

Some things I've learned on the journey....

I have learned to embrace my differences and the differences in others! I have learned that my differences will not allow me to connect with any and every one. I remember working so hard to establish and maintain friendships and relationships, which were life draining. In order for these relationships to be sustained I had to dumb down, compromise or tolerate unwanted behaviors, but the greatest was having the capacity to accept others as they were and being able to build them, without these same people having the capacity to accept and build me. It was unrealistic of me and it is unfair to others to expect someone to be all things to all people. Im done!

I have learned that disconnecting is and can be healthy when you've allowed yourself to choose you and take ownership of the types of relationships you want to have in your life! It's perfectly fine to be selective.

I've learned that you cannot have a thriving friendship with those who cloak envy, jealousy and resentment in admiration.

I've learned that me being GREAT doesn't make others inferior. Me being big doesn't make others small, but I can't do anything about how others feel about themselves in my presence.

I've learned that popularity does not equate to power. The in crowd is usually the most empty and dysfunctional. Being made separate is not a sentence but a selection!

I've learned that boundaries are necessary and sometimes that manifests as a closed door! Leave it closed!

I've learned to respect people's preferences, even if it's not me; but to never take it as a personal affront to who I am.

I've learned that some mistakes will never be forgiven or forgotten, and no matter how much evolution takes place, some will accept the new and others will hold fast to the old.

I've learned to LOVE despite "your" response- my wholeness is my responsibility alone.

I've learned to acknowledge, accept and act accordingly!

I've learned to release the past, love the present and harness the future.

I've learned to cultivate, activate and participate in environments that breed life and stimulate my core.

I never asked God to make me who I am, but since he did and did it well, I've learned to stop apologizing for it.

Me being me is always the best me! The greatness in me does not compete with the greatness in you!

-Pages of my Journal

We are truly better together! Our differences compliment and should collaborate rather than conquer and divide. In times of great need, great men and women rise to serve the greater purpose, even in adversity!

Consider great historical physicians, artists, philanthropists, authors. Often their journey to greatness is accompanied by monologues of times of uncertainty and disenchantment. Yet, their impact and influence upon the earth was substantial! If God did it for them, certainly if you believe, it has been done for you.

Disrobe! Take off the garments of fear, low self- esteem, limitation and restrictions. Disrobe! Throw away the clothing of your past mishaps, mistakes. Change your garments and put on the garments of righteousness and praise. Dress yourself in the garments of destiny and purpose! You have a wardrobe full of possibilities. Dress now for where you are going, not for where you have been!

In Jesus name I renounce, reject and disannul any agreement you have made with fear, intimidation, doubt and comparison. This is your time! Come out from the shadows, leave the cave, and embrace the open space you've been graced with. Step out from among the "common" and dare to confound the wise with wondrous works! You can do this. God is for you!

Take your eyes off the floor and look toward heaven! Go for it!

LEAD. DOMINATE. REIGN. PUSH. CREATE. PURSUE. DREAM. TRY AGAIN. ALL FAITH NO FEAR! DECLARE & DECREE! START THAT BUSINESS. GO BACK TO SCHOOL. WRITE THAT BOOK. RECORD THAT CD. PURCHASE THAT LAND. BUILD THE KINGDOM!

Just as God was with Moses, so he is with YOU! SHINE BRIGHT! IT'S YOUR TIME!

GO BE GREAT and be great with JOY!

15 Joy IN THE RAIN ...is a part of the JOURNEY.

Night never lasts. Good Morning Joy!

Conquering Cancer with Mom

I am the oldest child and the weight of my family had always been on my shoulders. Finally everyone was grown and settled. My son had left for college in September of 2018 and I had plans to travel or live internationally for a few months to promote the global vision of my non-profit ICM International Inc.

A few months later, in December of 2018, my entire life changed. My mother was diagnosed with terminal, stage 4 Breast Cancer. The cancer had literally spread throughout her body including behind the eyes. Rather than living what I had planned, I was told to make plans for end of life as this form of cancer did not have a cure and my Mother's chances of survival were next to none.

In a matter of days, we were thrusted into the greatest war we've ever known. The battle of life or death, and we chose life!

Although we believe the report of the Lord, the diagnosis catapulted my family into a state of emergency. Hospital stays, treatments, doctor appointments are merely the tip of the iceberg.

God has been my source of comfort and strength! Often I thought to cry, and just as often, he would not allow. Instead, He has engulfed me with JOY and laughter in this journey!

I began to fast and pray and the Lord speaks, "Come off your job. Trust me with the rest."

"Please God, not now. I need some stability more than ever now." It's funny how sometimes we think to know more and better for ourselves than he does. He responded, "Do you trust me? Come off the job."

That day, I resigned from being a corporate manager for state government and enlisted as one of my mother's caretakers. I knew this season of my life would require that not only I be a faith walker but a water walker as well. I knew I would never be the same. He had given me grace to leave the job, grace to trust him in this unfamiliar place and the grace to walk on water. I was given another opportunity to leap out of the boat once more, but this time with my Mother. His peace accompanied his word and calmed the storms surrounding me!

I leaped. This time I took the leap of faith by faith that I can do all things through Christ who strengthens me, with faith that I would see the goodness of the Lord in the land of the living, in faith that my mother would live and not die, through faith he would keep me in perfect peace if I kept my mind stayed on him, hoping against hope and believing that miracles, signs and wonders follow them that believe!

I believe God for the life of my mother and for the life of my destiny.

At the time of writing this book, I continue to endure with JOY, knowing death is not my Mother's portion and that he will sustain me in every area needed! God is yet performing miracles on our behalf. When the doctor said no, God said yes and not yet! We are living and believe for her complete healing! Whose report will you believe?

Seven months after diagnosis and we are yet prospering! I have observed my mother live on purpose. Her latest report indicated that there is no longer any cancer in the brain, no cancer in the organs, and for that we give

PRAISE! We are yet standing in agreement and have received by faith the finished work! In Jesus name her bones are cancer free, her occipital nerves are cancer free and she will live and be full of many days. With long life shall she live and be satisfied .We shall live healthy and prosper free of pestilence and disease and the curse of cancer is severed, broken and never to return! We are blessed! I am blessed!

He's never left me before, and he won't leave me now! I have Joy in the journey! I am fully persuaded that the testimony in totality will be healed and restored! We have won the victory!

So, What About this RAIN?

The little nursery rhyme "rain rain, go away, come again another day" seems befitting when you consider the dreary clouds that precede the tears of the sky. However, I now understand that rain is to be celebrated when you have seed in the ground! They that sow in tears shall indeed reap in JOY!

MY TEARS WERE SEED!

I remember playing in the rain as a kid and absolutely loved it! Somehow being wet in dry clothes is no longer appealing!! But I had a fascinating dream that might have changed this sentiment. Months ago I dreamt of rain falling in unprecedented amounts, drenching me from head to toe and I was fully clothed. The rain was falling so heavy that I couldn't discriminate between my fingers and the rain drops. I took a breath and breathed in the rain.

My lungs took in the water as if it were air. I could feel them expanding and contracting with ease. Obviously it is unnatural and impossible to breathe in that much water without suffocation or choking, however it seemed very normal. After waking, I really didn't think much of it because it has been raining heavily in the city, to the point of flooding. The next day I opened my bible with the intent to study about "rest" and my eye landed on this specific scripture;

1 Kings 18:41

King James Version

"And Elijah said unto Ahab, Get thee up, eat and drink; for there is a sound of abundance of rain".

New American Standard Bible says
"Now Elijah said to Ahab, "Go up, eat and drink; for there is the sound of the roar of a heavy shower."

The next day I was notified that there had been some damage to my office due to a leak in the roof as a result of the "heavy" shower of rain. I arrive at work to find the ceiling tile had fallen to the floor, insulation soaked and the duck work & roof exposed.

Ok Lord, you are trying to tell me something! It was then that I realized it's raining... drip drop, the ceiling is about to drop! In the spirit! Every barrier, limitation, blockade and cyclical wall is giving way to the rain! For so long many of you have been praying for the rain, expecting the rain, preparing for the rain. It's here! You are fully clothed and are about to get soaked! There is love, joy, provision, establishment and settlement in this rain. The Love of God is the motion that's causing this rain to fall and his unmerited favor is like the coolness of each drop!

In the word of God, water and even rain are symbolic to life, refreshing, nourishment, increase, newness, purity, holiness and cleansing! You've cried many tears but your weeping days are over. Joy is here!

I love this scripture:

Isaiah 35 1:7 NIV

Joy of the Redeemed

35 The desert and the parched land will be glad;
    the wilderness will rejoice and blossom.
Like the crocus, 2 it will burst into bloom;
    it will rejoice greatly and shout for joy.
The glory of Lebanon will be given to it,
    the splendor of Carmel and Sharon;
they will see the glory of the Lord,
    the splendor of our God.

3 Strengthen the feeble hands,
    steady the knees that give way;
4 say to those with fearful hearts,
    "Be strong, do not fear;
your God will come,
    he will come with vengeance;
with divine retribution
    he will come to save you."

5 Then will the eyes of the blind be opened
   and the ears of the deaf unstopped.
6 Then will the lame leap like a deer,
   and the mute tongue shout for joy.
Water will gush forth in the wilderness
   and streams in the desert.
7 The burning sand will become a pool,
   the thirsty ground bubbling springs.
In the haunts where jackals once lay,
   grass and reeds and papyrus will grow.

The bible indicates three seasons of rain:

- Latter rain- Melqosh – March to April
- Former/Early rain- Yoreh- (as known as Fall rains) Oct-November
- The Heavy rains/Winter Rains- Geshem- Dec-March

These rains- Yoreh- rains of the former come to supply the harvest its boost for maturity prior to it being gathered. Harvest is here but before you gather you must mature! The seed must mature, the crop must mature and that happens with the sun, the winds and the rain! There were many areas in my life that needed maturing in order for me to adequately possess the promises of God. I needed to GROW UP and grow into the woman I have become today. Maturing is not available by way of quick fix. Every hardship, every pinch and pull, every valley served as a force of nature that I might sprout into womanhood!

Rains of maturing are saturated with accountability, forgiveness, responsibility, discipline, diligence, stewardship, learning, humility, reciprocity, sharpening, pruning, purging, honesty, challenges as well as celebrations.

There were many opportunities for growth that I forfeited because they were clothed in "work"! At the time, I wasn't ready to commit to the level of work required to pull up and uproot weeds that were choking out good seeds. When rain falls it waters whatever is planted, good or bad!

You will not miss the next seasons outpouring of rain!

2 Kings 3:16-17- King Jehoshaphat finds himself between a rock and a hard place being lead into a valley. It's called the Valley of Ahsy. Ashy was rocky, deep, difficult terrain to navigate. They had travelled seven days fatigued, deprived, dehydrated from the journey but they had to travel there to confront an enemy long gone unaddressed. I have learned that there are seasons where we are led into the valley to defeat our enemy! He was led to the Valley, to overcome his enemy the Moabites. Those of us who are in the valley, might have been LED there. David defeated Goliath in the valley. Abrahams name was changed in the valley. Sara conceived in the valley while on the other hand Mary gave birth in the valley. Jesus himself was tempted in the Valley (the wilderness).

One of my favorite passages is when Jehoshaphat consults the prophet Elisha, and the prophet tells him to make the valley FULL of ditches.

> "Make this valley full of ditches, ye shall not see wind, neither rain YET that valley shall be filled w/ water, that you will drink both ye, your cattle & beasts.

MAKE this VALLEY FULL OF DITCHES... I meditated on what that might mean for me and others facing times of pressing...

MAKE an unfavorable circumstance, work in your favor!

The valley is not conducive to hold water but rather to allow water to run off which is why the valley is often associated or described as with being parched, dry and a low plain. Ditches receive and retain the water. In this instance, if it were to rain in the valley, the valley would swell or flood but the water would quickly disperse downward. Anybody receive "rain" in a past season or a blessing and just as quickly as you received it, was just as quickly you lost it? Something slipped through your hands last season. You missed out on some things last season. Some things went south/downward.

He said build the ditches! This rain you will receive and retain. You won't' see it but you will RECEIVE IT! Prepare and make room in the low place to receive and retain what's being released from the high place! Supernaturally you can go to bed in one condition and rise up overnight in another! I believe that you can go to bed poor and wake up rich! From sick to healed, empty to full, unemployed to employed! God is able!

And now let the weak say I am strong and let the poor say I am rich, from strength to strength! The Lord commanded you to receive the rain!

Who passing through the valley of Baca make it a well, the rain also filleth with pools. They go from strength to strength every one of them in Zion appeareth before God. Reference (Psalm 84:6-7)

Make Room for the RAIN!

Then I will send rain on your land in its season, both autumn and spring rains, so that you may gather in your grain, new wine and olive oil. (Deut. 11:4)

The Rain is coming!

Psalm 107: 35-38 Says "He changes a wilderness into a pool of water, and a dry land into springs of water and there (in the dry land) he makes the hungry to dwell, so that they may establish an inhabited city; and sow field and plant vineyards and gather fruitful harvest, also he blesses them and they multiply greatly, he does not let their cattle decrease.

He pours water on ground that is thirsty. Rain is only important to those who have seed in the ground and are thirsty! Those that expect God's blessing must prepare ROOM for them. I decree there is room in you! Pour in Father! You are a well ready to receive the rain with Joy!

Abraham had built wells to retain water for his livelihood and his cattle and when he died the Philistines stopped up the well. His son Isaac goes to unstop the well and sees that the wells weren't dry after all but rather COVERED- BLOCKED- HINDERED. He met much opposition in uncovering the well, but God supplied. If you are feeling dry, ask yourself, "Am I dry or am I stopped up?" Dry or stopped, there is an answer! Could it be you're not dry at all, you're just stopped up! It's time to uncover the well within.

Our Father specializes in refreshing, replenishing, reviving and restoring!

I call forth the rain of heaven to be released in Jesus name! I encourage you to prepare to dance in the rain! Morning has come and so has your ***JOY!***

Love you always,

Remember Joy overall is yours!

ABOUT THE AUTHOR

Inspirational speaker, Shaylon Ware embodies a keen transparency that comes from an authentic candidness that ignites, heals, and transforms lives across the globe. Her profound revelatory messages are empowering, provoking and unconventional; inspiring individuals to embrace their identity with untamed purpose. A multi-dimensional woman of faith, vision, passion and purpose, Shaylon Ware is dedicated to building, leading and empowering through inspiration, biblical truth, and transformation.

Apostle Shaylon Ware (Shaylon Ware Global ministries) is a nationally and internationally recognized anointed preacher of the gospel, empowerment speaker, prophetic worship leader, author and humanitarian who has a heart for mankind. She is vibrant, bold, innovative community leader who is highly sought after, having facilitated workshops, training, and conferences for kingdom advancement. By grace she has served in Ghana West Africa, the Dominican Republic, Anquilla, West Antilles and a host of states.

The Apostolic mandate upon her life is to equip, lead and empower kingdom leaders. She is the CEO & Founder of ICM International Inc. - a nonprofit (501c3) Apostolic Hub that provides training, development & resource services in the areas of mentorship, ministry, and missions; as well as a triple entrepreneur (Shaylon Ware Enterprise) *Untamed*, an empowerment, counseling, and consulting firm. Her multifaceted approach in engaging and capturing an audience is a direct result of her faith and vested purpose to encourage, empower and edify.

Shaylon Ware serves in leadership for the Government of Washington, DC and a certified counselor of more than 15 years. She has a bachelor's degree in Deafness Rehabilitation and a master's degree in Rehabilitation Counseling from Northern Illinois University, combined with nearly 20 years of corporate government leadership and program management. She is the proud Mother of one son, Jalen Wilson, and resides in Washington, DC.

TESTIMONYs OF JOY IN THE JOURNEY

TESTIMONY

I was born 05-08-1949. Growing up I always liked being with my elders, especially my grandmothers. There was an elderly cousin I used to love to visit. I would play on her back porch. This is where I had my first spiritual experience. I didn't know that's what it was at the time. I heard someone call me and I went to her and she said it wasn't her calling me. This happened a second and a third time. Finally, the third time I went to her she told me that it was death that was calling me, and it scared me. I later realized it was the Lord. At age 8 or 9 my dad's mother prayed for me often. Even as a wild teenager, I never wanted to play with God. My desire was to be real. At 17 I was saved and it changed me and was married at 18. I didn't know about being spirit filled but my grandmother did her best to teach me. At age 24 I was filled with the Holy Spirit. My marriage was in big trouble but I remember crying out to God to help me. I couldn't help myself and he was my answer.

I found him to be faithful. I have had many experiences with him from dreams to smells, people crossing my path when I was being tested and tried. He would manifest himself and always showed himself to be true. I learned how true the scripture that said God is not man that he should lie. The love of God will sustain you through infidelities, sickness, poverty, discouragement. Whatever may come, I have learned to look to the Lord and speak the word. I always knew that there was no failure in God. If there was a problem, I had to check to see if I was that problem. I wasn't perfect. I worked at Maybelline for 22 years and I did my best to glorify God. I promised him if I got a job I would share Jesus with those around me. When I did, I wasn't always received. My largest conflict would come from other Christians. There were many battles I didn't win but I never gave up on him, it would be like saying God can't do it. Even in trials now, the same rules apply. Philippians 1:6 I am sure of this that he who has begun a good work in you will complete. These words have meant so much to me. There is so much more but it's all in him.

Sincerely,

Henryetta Anderson

TESTIMONY

I thank God for the journey and the joy that comes with knowing he holds me in his hands. His eyes are on the sparrow, I know he watches me. True joy comes with being fully persuaded that he is able to keep that, that I commit to him. He keeps me (Romans 14:5).

The bible says many are the afflictions of the righteous but he would deliver us out of them all. I trust him with me. Sometimes on this journey you have to go through somethings; you have to remember you are going through, not staying. I remember once going through a trial, one of the coldest winters Arkansas had seen. I was pregnant, husband unemployed, living in the housing project, gas was cut off and ice sickles were hanging inside and outside my kitchen window. We were confined to one small bedroom with a heater and two other children. I was praying, thinking God what did I do to make you this angry with me. Please forgive me and tell me so I'll never do it again. He told me to read Philippians 4:12. He said, "Deon you've done nothing wrong. He then said, "Look around, the children are full, warm, playing and you are not suffering. You are inconvenienced but you have food in the pantry. Learn how to abound and to be abased. Suffer need. One day you will be able to use this as a testimony. Everything you go through is not because you've done something or punishment, but for ministry sake that I might know him.

He delivered me that very day; not out of what I was going through, but my spirit man was filled with so much joy because he loved me and trusted me with this trial. I was determined to wait until my change came and it did. A few months after that he blessed me with my own home!

I have gone through many things on this journey of life. It has taught me to know him in a real way. Now I can tell the world he is real with confidence. He's been a lawyer in a courtroom, a doctor when they said I wouldn't make it. I've had my heart broken and he's mended it. He kept my mind when I would have lost it and made a way when there was no way. I've seen miracles (Hallelujah!). I wouldn't take anything from my journey.

My prayer for you dearest readers is that you may know him and the power of his might. That's real joy in the journey!

God bless every one of you.

Sincerely,

Aunt Deon Allen